Pearson's Canal Comp[anion]
PENNINE WAT[ERS]

Published by J.M.Pearson & Son Ltd, Tatenhill Common, Staffordshire DE13 9RS Tel/fax 01283 713674

Copyright: Michael Pearson - All rights reserved. First edition 1995. ISBN 0 907864 69 4

Printed by Clifford Press of Coventry in associaton with the Portfolio Press of Barnoldswick

INTRODUCTION

COMPILATION of this guide began in rain - a sodden walk from Wigan to Chorley rendering me so comprehensively wet that I left a pool of water on the seat of the train home - and ended in sunshine - with Jackie at the "Pool Court", Leeds, sipping celebratory aperitifs on a balcony overhanging the Aire. In between, nine months of walking, cycling, boating and motoring; of growing familiarity with places as distinct and diverse as Blackburn, Bingley and Burnley, Walsden, Woodlesford and Wakefield. In between, nine months of research and writing, cartography and photography, fact-checking and phrase-polishing. And 'in between' Wigan and the outskirts of Rochdale, by way of Leeds, 146 miles of navigable waterway and walkable towpath which I came to regard with unshakable affection; wondering why we had waited so long to include these "Pennine Waters" in the Canal Companion series.

Wondering why? It was no mystery to us. We reckoned these waters so underboated as to render any guide published specifically to cover them unviable. The canals of the North are in a different league from their mellow Midland cousins. But they are not as intimidating as received wisdom suggests. And, in any case, the toughest nuts to crack are invariably the tastiest in the pack. So we urge you to go and explore these canals, and not only in order to maximise our profits. They are on the verge of popularity, and you know how vulgar that can be. Get there before the crowds and you may still relish, as we did, the grandeur of their loneliness.

Michael Pearson

Oddy Two

BLACK Prince

NARROWBOAT
HOLIDAYS

Life in the Slow Lane

FORGET THE CROWDS
find a new life with

SHIRE CRUISERS

The Wharf, Sowerby Bridge HX6 2AG. Tel: 01422-832712 Fax: 01422-839565

Holiday Boat Hire • Moorings • Boat Repairs • Engine Service • Gas • Diesel • Pumpout • Shop

From Manchester ("Cheshire Ring")

From Liverpool

Wigan

Girobank

WHETHER Wigan marks the beginning, or the end, of your exploration of the canals of the Pennines, it is not the kind of place that can be easily erased from your memory. If there is a more gruelling flight of locks in the country, it does not spring readily to mind. Not only does each chamber consist of four heavily mitred gates, but each of six sets of paddle gear (two ground, four gate) is hand-cuff locked as a security measure against vandalism. Neither does the surrounding 'scenery' offer much by way of compensation, let alone inspiration. What! No inspiration in Wigan's canalscape of wastegrounds, terraced housing and abandoned factories? Have Pearsons gone soft? No, of course not, this is just the equivalent of a 'government health warning', and the subtext reads:"if you like your canals green and rural, then steer clear of Wigan!"

But, of course, you're not

going to. Like us, you've come, and seen, and been conquered by Wigan's uncondescending charm. True North - True Grit. Let's get this show on the road!

In our CHESHIRE RING Canal Companion we awoke imagining the sound of clogs on cobbles at Wigan Pier, and that seems as good a point as any to begin this Pennine Journey. Leaving astern Wigan's heartland of textile mills, the Leeds & Liverpool Canal's main line passes the junction of its branch to Leigh (and thence the Bridgewater Canal link with Manchester) and commences a climb in excess of two hundred feet in less than two miles up to the level of the old Lancaster Canal.

Railway bridges frame the first lock - the eighty-fifth from Leeds, but twenty-first from the top - which sets the tone for the whole flight. Expect to take at least four hours in a boat with an experienced crew; though you can ask BW for help if you could do with some extra muscle, or are simply of a nervous disposition.

Steadily you begin to accumulate locks under your belt. In the momentum of your journey they begin to lose individuality. Little streets with the whiff of the 19th century about them overlook the canal between locks 80 and 81, whilst in the following pound, neat new industrial units provoke piquant contrast with the sooty walls of an old works beyond. The past cannot be so easily expunged. Bat an eyelid, and a 'Wiganer' might easily glide out of the next chamber loaded to the gunnels with

WIGAN

1 The Way We Were
2 The Orwell
3 Museum Shop
4 Terminal Warehouse
5 Wigan Pier
6 Trencherfield Mill

Pottery Road

Walgate

BW

Town Centre

Wigan Locks No.s 65-87 214ft 7ins

Wigan Bakery

golf course

Haigh Hall Country Park

"Crawford Arms"

Red Rock

B5239

B5239 to Standish

B5238 to Aspull

coal. Overnight moorings are provided between locks 77 and 78 if you're caught in mid flight, so to speak, in an area of new housing where the canal environment has been refurbished with a tiled towpath and neatly grassed verge. Such cosmetic improvements provide a metaphor for Wigan itself: lean, gaunt and partially refurbished. Still, at Lock 73 - overlooked by a high slag heap which can be scrambled up for panoramic views over Wigan - the trackbed of the old Lancashire Union Railway has been converted into a creditable footpath signposted "Haigh Country Park". Bridge 56 is inscribed '1816' and gives access to Kirkless Hall, a partially half-timbered farmhouse presumably predating the industrialism of Wigan.

A pair of canalside pubs make a welcome sight as the flight reaches its logical conclusion. Top Lock is also known as Aspull Lock. It is overlooked by a lock-keeper's cottage, a small office and, to the rear, old stabling. Facilities include water, Elsan and refuse disposal and public toilets. Spend a few minutes exploring. Go and gaze over the parapet of bridge 59, along what was to have been the line of the Lancaster Canal on its way to join the Bridgewater at Westhoughton near Worsley, before the money ran out. But be advised not to moor overnight unless there are other boats here. Far better to summon one last gasp of energy and proceed to (or stop short at) Red Rock where much more salubrious visitor moorings are provided alongside the congenial "Crawford Arms".

Journeying eastwards (though north-west at first) urban Wigan is quickly exchanged for a predominantly rural landscape, there being no development beyond the B5238. By bridge 59A there are suggestions of a former wharf and, nearby, a curiously bell-towered stone house. The canal rides along a low escarpment providing views westwards as far as the cooling towers of Fiddlers Ferry power station on the banks of the Mersey. The grounds of Haigh Hall spill down to the waterside. There is a serene passage through woodland, with an elegant footbridge throwing its graceful, lattice, paint-flaking span over the cut adjacent to a small reedy basin replete with stone side bridge, probably provided for goods destined for use at the hall. Haigh Hall itself is now a municipal amenity, more or less masked by trees beyond a golf course which accompanies the canal for some way.

Water lilies thrive in the vicinity of bridge 61. At RED ROCK the main Euston-Glasgow railway is momentarily visible in the valley of the Douglas, and the spire of Standish church punctures the horizon. Pleasant visitor moorings are provided to the north of bridge 63 where there are remains of an old coal tippler. The hillsides beyond the river were once extensively opencast mined and presumably the canal accommodated some of this trade.

Wigan 21

OCK-free, and crossing the boundary between Greater Manchester and Lancashire, the 'Lancaster Pool' essays a serpentine course, revelling in peaceful countryside, with many stretches richly wooded.

Arley Hall, now a golf clubhouse, is surrounded by a moat. Red House Aqueduct carries the canal across the River Douglas. After rain (and by gum did it rain when we came along here) the river water gushed down between its high banks like the charge of the Light Brigade. The extensive White Bear Marina occupies the site of White Bear railway station, whilst the painted gable end of the old Adlington Industrial Co-op Bakery mournfully overlooks a small, canalside park provided with useful visitor moorings.

ADLINGTON itself introduces some welcome variety to the canal's woodland wanderings.

To the east, Pennine moorlands rise up in waves of Lowry-like loneliness and solitude-evoking imagery. The tower on Rivington Pike is backed by Winter Hill and its radio masts. Pike Tower has been an East Lancashire landmark since it was erected in the 18th century. It stands on a summit 1200ft above sea level and on a clear day you can see the Isle of Man from here. For a number of years it belonged to Lord Leverhulme of "Sunlight Soap" fame. A fell-runners' race to the Pike takes place every Easter Saturday.

Another boatyard, squeezed into a narrow cutting alongside the A6 trunk road from London to Carlisle, brings activity to the canal in the vicinity of Heath Charnock. The course of an abandoned railway leads to the site of Duxbury Park and Ellerbeck collieries. The former was closed by its owners during the Depression before being rescued and re-opened by its workforce; a scenario which seems vaguely familiar. Ellerbeck pit remained open until 1965. So much coal was carried along the canal that, when the water was drained for maintenance, local people would rush out and pick (or 'kebb' in the local vernacular) any spilt coal from the bed of the canal.

Oblivious to the canal, and just about everything else, Michael Pearson staggered through Adlington one Saturday afternoon in 1973 on the "Bogle Stroll", a 50 mile charity walk along the A6 from Lancaster to Manchester. Unfortunately, like the Lancaster Canal itself, he ran out of resources in the neighbourhood of Westhoughton, 10 miles short.

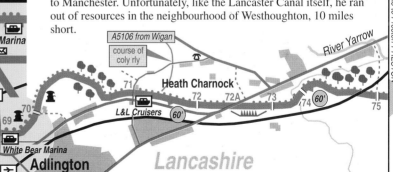

Johnson's Hillock

*T*HE canal treats Chorley rather disdainfully, skirting the eastern rim of the town, so that all the inland navigator gets to see is a periphery of mills and housing estates. The M61 inveigles its way into the landscape, but you can lift up your eyes to the serene wooded top of Healey Nab and the wuthering heights of Anglezark Moor beyond.

JOHNSON'S HILLOCK LOCKS may be a bit tongue-twisting, but they combine to create a gorgeous flight of seven chambers, carrying the 'real' Leeds & Liverpool Canal down to (or up from) the Lancaster Canal's original route. Setting off in the direction of its old summit at Walton, the Lancaster peters out in the vicinity of Whittle-le-Woods, a good deal of its course having been submerged beneath the M61. At Walton cargoes were transhipped from barge on to tramway wagons and taken across the steeply-sided Ribble Valley before being arduously floated once again at Preston Basin.

But back to the delights of Johnson's Hillock, where the immaculately coiffeured chambers are separated, each from the other - towards the foot of the flight at least - by broad glassy pools. A grassy path winds through buttercup and clover meadows grazed by congenial geldings on the offside, crossing by-weirs on neat little timber footbridges which contribute much to the beauty of the scene.

Above the locks, the canal curves around the steep-sided valley of the River Lostock. Banks of gorse line the cut. Herons patrol their beats along the canal bank. Rolling sheep pastures and ribbons of woodland combine to create a soothing landscape for the canal to lose itself in. Peace reigns supreme in what amounts to a surprising vacuum of agricultural land between the old textile centres of East Lancs.

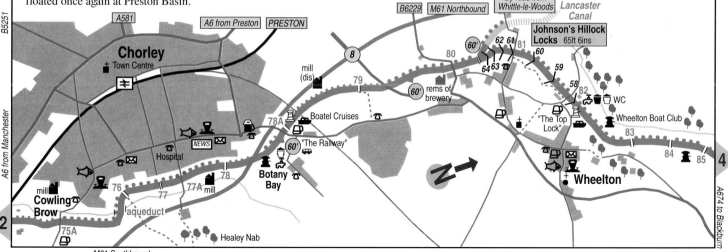

CROSSING the watershed between the rivers Lostock and Darwen - both tributaries of the Ribble, though not destined to meet before the estuary - the canal traverses a largely rural landscape whose only brush with urbanisation is the suburbs of Feniscowles. By bridge 87 a steep sided clough all but hides an enigmatic, high-vaulted bridge which might almost be carrying a second canal. No other guide, past or present, we could lay our hands on, even mentions it. Trust Pearsons to have the facts at their fingertips! It's the Thirlmere water supply aqueduct, opened in 1894 to bring water a hundred miles from the Lake District to Manchester.

As publishers, papermaking is a subject close to our hearts, though it is hardly any longer a significant facet of British Industry. Many mills have closed. Those that haven't tend to be in foreign ownership. East Lancs was a notable centre of papermaking and the Leeds & Liverpool played an important role in transporting raw materials and fuel to the works and the finished product away. These days the canal reflects metaphorically - and sometimes quite literally - the fickle fortunes of the paper industry. At WITHNELL FOLD a mill which once produced bank-note paper for currencies throughout the civilized world has been colonised by sundry light industries. Forty-eight hour visitor moorings exist in the shadow of the mill and you could well fill those hours exploring the vicinity of this charming backwater. Beyond the towpath wall the land falls suddenly away to a series of filter beds which have been transformed into a nature reserve, a primeval paradise of dragonflies, water lilies and dipping pools. In the opposite direction a stroll up the cobbled lane from bridge 88 introduces you to a 'model' village of paper-workers' cottages and a piquant little green with a sundial as its centrepiece; a moving memorial to the local men who didn't march home from two world wars.

Near Riley Green the M65's controversial link with the M6 was nearing completion - 'tree-people' notwithstanding - as we passed. At Bridge 91A a modern pub and boatyard occupy the site of an old short-boat building yard. The paper industry rears its high-chimnied head again between bridges 92 and 93B. Coal came in by barge and you can still see the mooring rings and evidence of an aerial ropeway employed to carry the coal from the canal bank into the works.

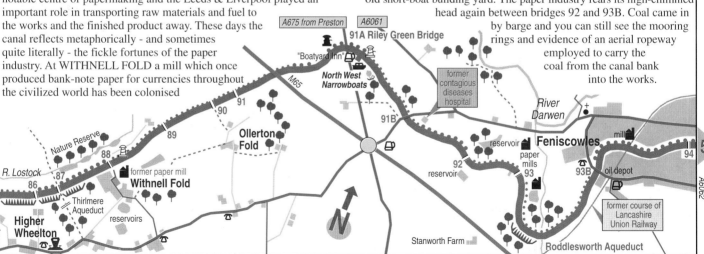

Withnell Fold

BLACKBURN impinges its urban - though not necessarily urbane - personality on the canal, obliterating all sense of countryside for the best part of five miles. There are still, however, green horizons to savour: Jubilee Tower on Darwen Hill to the south; the woodlands of Witton Country Park to the north. But this is primarily a part of the journey which should be devoted to disinterring the remains of King Cotton; though it must be emphasised that the local authority have not been content to live in the past, and a good deal of work has been undertaken to revitalise Blackburn's canal corridor: if only the hooligans would refrain from vandalising the improvements the moment that they are made.

Every Sixties adolescent remembers from 'Sgt. Pepper' that there were "Four thousand holes in Blackburn, Lancashire." But once there were two hundred factory chimneys as well, one of them, at 312ft, probably the highest in the UK, stood canalside at Bennington Street refuse works, built in 1888 of nearby Accrington's famously durable bricks. Durable, but dynamitable, and now you can count Blackburn's post industrial smoke stacks on your fingers. Many mills have shuffled their mortal coil too, or found new uses - a pub in the Albion, television news studios at Daisyfield - but pride of place remains with the massive Imperial Mill by bridge 104A, a vast, sprawling, redbrick, zinc-domed dinosaur hanging on for dear life pending possible refurbishment as a heritage attraction and business centre under the auspices of Blackburn's "City Challenge" scheme. In 1910 there were 87,377 looms in the town operated by 42,000 dexterous textile workers,

Key

1 Nova Scotia Mills
2 Thwaite's Brewery
3 Daisyfield Mill
4 Imperial Mill
5 India Mill
6 Greenbank Mill
a site of Paradise Mills
b site of Gorse Bridge Mill
c site of Hole House Mill
d former Green Bank Iron Wks

Blackburn

PRESTON
A674
A6062
4

A677 from Preston
CLITHEROE
GT HARWOOD BURNLEY
6

Cherry Tree
Witton Country Park
school
River Darwen
95 eng wks
NEWS
96
Mill Hill
96A
NEWS
96B
Waterfall Mills
Moorgate Mill
Waterloo
97
98
Albion Mill
Ewood Park

NOVA SCOTIA WHARF
Blackburn Locks 52-57
54ft 9ins
99
56 55
100
54 53 52
99A
57
Hosp.
1

NOVA SCOTIA WHARF
60'
99 Lock-keeper
56
55
99A

Waves
mus
market
EANAM WHARF
Morrisons
Ice Arena
Asda
Tommy Balls
102A
102
site of incinerator chimney
103
103A

EANAM WHARF
Town Centre
Historic Warehouse
60'
103AA
103A

103A
103B
a
104
5 6
d site of Greenbank gas works
b
4
Tesco
104A c
104C
104B

A666 to Darwen BOLTON
A677 to Rossendale

many of them children as young as twelve.

Number-crunching still comes naturally to Blackburn. Crossing an embankment on the western edge of town, Ewood Park football stadium soars above humble terraced rooftops. Blackburn Rovers' history goes back much further than Jimmy Hill and "Match of the Day". They were First Division champions twice in the years leading up to the First World War, and FA Cup winners on six occasions, though not since 1928. The fallow years, however, are over with Kenny Dalglish ensconsed as manager and local steel magnate Jack Walker's cheque book underwriting the club's purchasing power on the transfer market. Upwards of £54 million has been invested to take Rovers to the top of the footballing tree, numbers as crunching as Colin Hendry's tackles, and in 1995 they became champions of the Premier League. If only the Leeds & Liverpool Canal had an equally munificent sugar daddy.

A flight of six locks carries the canal up on to its elevated position on the western edge of town. A lock-keeper resides at NOVA SCOTIA WHARF where the Groundwork Trust have refurbished former stables and workshops, and where the provision of water and refuse disposal provides boaters with reasonably secure moorings for a stopover in Blackburn. As we have observed before, local authorities should do more to provide boaters with reassuring facilities for overnight stays. In Blackburn's case, they represent the majority of tourist, as opposed to business, visitors to the town, and much more should be done to make them welcome. We were 'welcomed' at Eanam Wharf by a gentleman objecting to our mooring in front of his house. Wishing to avoid a local incident, we reversed beneath the warehouse canopy, tied-up alongside the wide boat "Kennet", and sought advice from the council office within. "Yes, you're OK to moor here, but you'll be locked in after four-thirty, unless you've got a BW handcuff key". We had; so, so far, so good. Then we discovered that it was only feasible to unlock the gate from the outside. Fortunately, we numbered amongst our crew, an exile from the Polish State Circus, agile enough to circumnavigate the wrought-iron 'security' fence and let us out. But what a palaver. Little wonder boaters think twice about stopping at Blackburn. In the event we spent a peaceful night, undisturbed until the arrival, at eight-thirty next morning, of the crew of a maintenance boat moored alongside (for

similar considerations of security) the evening before.

Overlooked by a plethora of mills, and providing a fascinating panoramic view of the town - notably its cathedral and Thwaite's brewery - the canal zig-zags around the eastern fringe of the centre. Audley Bridge (102A) appears to have been reinforced with girders cast as far afield as Darlington in 1878; perhaps with Blackburn's soon to be developed tramway system in mind. The trams are long gone, but the vast barn of a railway station survives. It must have been a showcase for 'The Lanky' at the turn of the century. Now it's a great ghost of lost causes and missed connections. The goods shed has become an indoor go-kart track, but the station still occasionally resounds to the steamy hoot of the 'Cumbrian Mountain Express' on its way to or from the fabled Settle & Carlisle.

Extensive coal wharves once abutted both sides of Cicely Street Bridge (103) and a travelling crane facilitated fast turnrounds for discharging barges. Tommy Ball's shoe emporium occupies the site of Alma cotton mill, access from the towpath being by way of a new footbridge spanning the canal at EANAM WHARF, one of the Leeds & Liverpool's most significant goods depots. Twenty-five thousand natives gathered to see its opening in 1810. The local rag's 'shipping list' for the 27th June of that year quotes the arrival of the barges "Dispatch" carrying yarn, molasses and tallow; "Defiance" with timber and lead; and "Ten Sisters" bearing malt and earthenware. A hundred and forty-five years later John Seymour arrived here aboard his converted Dutch sailing barge "Jenny the Third" ("Sailing Through England", Eyre & Spottiswoode 1956) and found the depot stuffed with cotton bales brought by lorry from Liverpool docks. For short boats, wide boats - call them what you will - the writing was already on the wall. Now the writing on the interior walls of the wharf's handsomely restored warehouse interprets Blackburn's rich canal heritage and its ramifications for the local economy.

Between bridges 103A and 104A the emphasis is overtly industrial. Paradise Bridge (103B) seems somewhat ironically named unless you are deeply into industrial archaeology. Evidence of the emasculation of heavy industry is evinced by bridge 104A where the Furthergate Chemical Works has become a Tesco superstore: the young turks of East Lancashire stacking shelves with artichokes and anchovies where their grandfathers superintended the production of chlorines and hydrocarbonates.

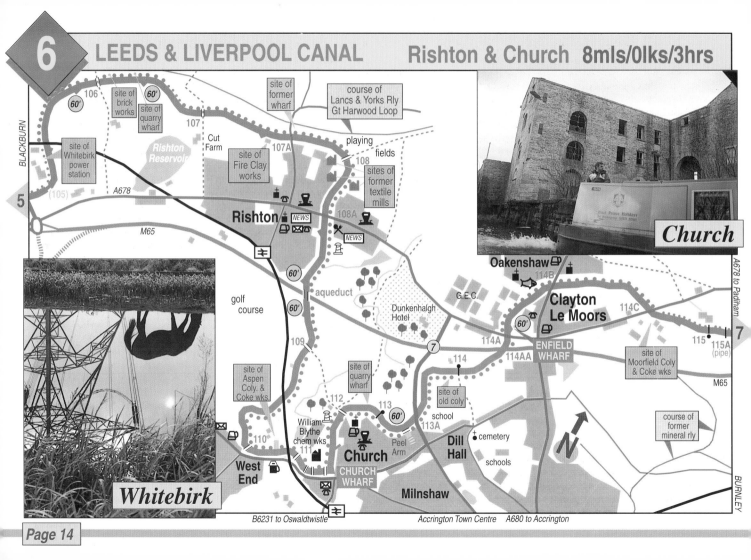

BLACKBURN

106   60'

site of brick works

60' site of quarry wharf

107

Cut Farm

site of Whitebirk power station

(105)

A678

Rishton Reservoir

site of former wharf

course of Lancs & Yorks Rly Gt Harwood Loop

playing fields

107A

site of Fire Clay works

108

5

M65

Rishton NEWS

108A

sites of former textile mills

NEWS

Church

60'

aqueduct

golf course

60'

Dunkenhalgh Hotel

G.E.C.

Oakenshaw

114B

Clayton Le Moors

114C

A678 to Padiham

7

109

7

114A

114AA

ENFIELD WHARF

60'

115   115A (pipe)

site of Moorfield Coly & Coke wks

M65

site of Aspen Coly. & Coke wks.

site of quarry wharf

114

site of old coly

school

113A

cemetery

schools

course of former mineral rly

N

112

113

60'

William Blythe chem wks

Peel Arm

Dill Hall

110

111

Church

West End

CHURCH WHARF

Milnshaw

Whitebirk

B6231 to Oswaldtwistle

Accrington Town Centre   A680 to Accrington

BURNLEY

CONTRIVING to double the crow-flying distance between Blackburn and Clayton, the Leeds & Liverpool curves voluptuously with the contours, the canal equivalent of a Renoir nude. In cargo-carrying days this profligacy with the miles may have irked, but now we are grateful for as much of this invigorating and stimulating canal journey as we can get; valuing its long-windedness, letting the Calder Valley motorway cater for the speed merchants.

Blackburn becomes a memory. A bland retail park replaces Whitebirk Power Station, source of the last regular trade on this section of the canal, until the thirteen-week freeze of '63 finally convinced the Electricity Generating Board of the inefficacy of canal transport. The power station had been built in 1921 on the site of a plantation. Coal was discharged from barges on the offside - a wasteground of saplings now - and conveyed overhead into the plant on the towpath side of the canal. The bulk of Whitebirk's coal came from Bank Hall Colliery at Burnley (a lockless 15 miles to the east), but a proportion also originated from pits in the Wigan coalfield. They stopped making the sparks fly here in 1976 and the power station was demolished seven years later.

Around the next bend quarrying brought traffic to the canal, tramways linking the cut with workfaces on the hillside. Evidence of such wharves remains along with ramps cut into the canal bank to simplify the recovery of boat horses which had fallen into the water. Rishton Reservoir was built in 1828 to augment water supplies to the western end of the canal. The Blackburn - Burnley railway crosses its southern end by causeway. The old loop line to Great Harwood closed to passenger trains in 1957. Canon Roger Lloyd, one of many clergymen with a deep interest in railways, wrote of it in "Farewell to Steam", recalling that when he was vicar at Great Harwood in the Twenties, 75% of the working population were unemployed and on the Means Test.

Exhilaratingly androgynous, the landscape combines the feminine allure of pastures backed by waves of moorland, with the masculinity of industry and urbanisation. Chameleon-like, the canal seems to alter its character and sexual persuasion in response to its environment. RISHTON is imbued with XY chromosomes, and though its gaunt mills have tumbled, tightly-packed terraced streets remain.

A concrete aqueduct carries the canal over the motorway. Down there on that tarmac they are travelling so rapidly that they can avoid the need to think altogether. Shunning this example, the canal traveller circumnavigates the community of CHURCH: though take to the path which swoops down into the Aspen valley between bridges 109 and 112 and you can beat the boat with ease. Now carried on an embankment, when the East Lancs Railway was built in 1848, the line crossed the valley on a lengthy timber viaduct. It took twenty years of spoil-tipping to bury the bridge. Aspen Colliery opened in 1869. Coke was produced in a series of 'beehive' ovens, traces of which remain beside a reed-filled basin adjacent to the railway. Once there were fifteen mines in the neighbourhood of Church and Oswaldtwistle. Chemical production is another local industry. William Blythe's are still flourishing a hundred and fifty years after the said Mr Blythe, a canny Scot from Kirkaldy, set up in business, attracted by the canal's transport potential.

A substantial, three-storey canal warehouse overlooks a right-angle bend in the canal at Church Wharf. Flyboats once unloaded cotton here, and despite the ruined state of the building, still seem almost tangible. St James's church marks the halfway point between Liverpool and Leeds. Eastbound boaters encounter their first swing-bridges: familiarity will breed not so much contempt as a deep and lasting loathing. There were proposals, towards the end of the 19th century, to extend the Peel Arm (dug initially to serve a calico works) into the centre of Accrington, but sadly (for Accrington is a fascinating place) they never came to fruition.

ENFIELD WHARF marked a hiatus in the canal's westbound construction for several years while more capital was raised. Now it's the lugubrious home to Hydburn Sea Scouts and its warehouses wait in vain for a new use. We looked in vain for Appleby's flour mill, operators, once, of a fleet of barges, and the soap factory which specialised in the production of 'floating soap'. Briefly rubbing shoulders with suburbia, the Leeds & Liverpool is soon out into open country east of Clayton, a community not quite so bucolic as its name implies. The comedian, Eric Morecambe, worked as a Bevan boy at Moorfield Colliery during the Second World War. Not so amusingly, the mine was the scene of an undergound explosion in 1883, causing the deaths of sixty-eight workers including boys as young as ten. Now its site, and that of the adjoining coke works, is being developed as an industrial estate.

Huncoat

YES, those are *green* fields lapping at the margins of the cut, stretching from the towpath's drystone wall boundary to a horizon of moorlands, the Calder Valley, Trough of Bowland and Pendle Hill. Savour them, for there is an inevitability about the onslaught of Burnley and Blackburn. As the prophet said: "Lift up thine eyes to the hills, but for heaven's sake don't bump into Clough Bank Bridge."

Southwards, beyond the tall chimney which is all that remains of Huncoat power station, the quarry-scalloped edge of Great Hameldon (1343ft) prefaces the lonely tops of the Forest of Rossendale. But the motorway effectively curtails the proximity of this landscape, and it is northwards, over the valley of the Calder (no relation to the navigable West Riding namesake, though born of the same watershead) that the canal traveller's eye tends to be drawn. We caught glimpses of a snow-capped Penyghent. In the middle distance the parkland demesnes of Read, Simonstone and Huntroyde contrast with stone-walled pastures patterned by darker masses of woodland, ascending to the mottled flanks of Pendleton Moor. Nearer at hand the canal arcs to cross a series of ravines, or cloughs as they call them

hereabouts, gouged out by watercourses cascading down to the Calder. In Altham Clough Wood old maps locate the existence of coal pits. And indeed, for such a comparatively rural setting, there is much for the diligent industrial archaeologist to uncover. The site, for example of Altham Vitriol Works; the enigmatic canalside ruin at Lower Clough Bank; the remains of Altham Brick & Tile Works; Castle Clough Dyeworks and the vanished Perseverance Mill at Hapton must all have stories to tell if only we had the space and the time.

Between Hapton and Rose Grove the canal was diverted to facilitate construction of the motorway. This end of the old Great Harwood Loop Line railway has only recently been lifted following the cessation of coal carrying to Padiham's now demolished power station. Rose Grove has railway resonances too, for here, on a site now largely buried beneath the M65, was one of the last three motive power depots retained to service steam until August 1968. The locomotives took their water from the canal, and it was said that they could always tell a Rose Grove tender when it went to the works by the shoals of minnows inside. British Waterways have a maintenance base in a handsomely restored warehouse by bridge 126A.

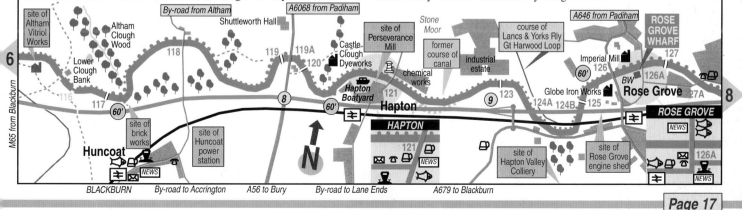

GANNOW TUNNEL

Plover Street

Tunnel Street

NEWS

M65

L IKE a custom-officer slamming a hairy fist down on your passport, Burnley embosses a distinct impression on the Leeds & Liverpool Canal as it curves coruscatingly from one fresh view to another, seemingly determined to disembowel Burnley and pick over its entrails. And entrails don't come much juicier to predatory industrial archaeologists than the textile town's famous Weaver's Triangle, a dense conglomerate of mills and weaving sheds gathered on the banks of the waterway which kick-started its 19th century zenith of prosperity. Between bridges 129B and 130B the canal is at its most scintillating as it weaves - forgive the pun - between man-made canyons of lofty mills. Of unique interest, are the premises by bridge 130

A679 from Blackburn BLACKBURN

7

127B
127C

A671 from Whalley

GANNOW TUNNEL

(10)

1

2

129 aqueduct

Burnley Barracks

Weaver's Triangle

3
4
5
129B
130
6

viaduct

(11)

Central

River Calder

site of Clifton Colliery

site of Reedley Colliery

133
134
135
132A
132
park
mill shop
(60')

131B
131A
gasholder
9
a
8
NEWS
131

school

M'chester Road
(60')
130B

BURNLEY WHARF
i
Recreation Centre
Sainsbury

7
Superbowl

FINSLEY GATE YARD

130C
130D
130E

130A

Burnley
River Brun
park

aqueduct

BURNLEY EMBANKMENT
130H

Turf Moor Burnley F.C.

River Calder

site of Bank Hall Colliery

(60')

M65

B6248 from Fence

136
137 138
(60')
gasholder
e
c
d
139

Pendle Water

Industrial Estate

(12)

Brierfield

By-road to Widdop Moor

Little Marsden

COLNE

9

Oaks Hotel Reedley

BURNLEY

130B Historic Warehouse
■ Visitor Centre
Manchester Road

130C

130D

130E

Centenary Way

Town Centre

Superbowl

Finsley Gate

BURNLEY EMBANKMENT

Belfields

BRIERFIELD

137

"Railway Tavern"

A682

Key

1 site of Cairo & Albion mills
2 Olive mount Mill
3 Woodfield Mill 1888
4 Victoria Mill 1855
5 Slater Terrace
6 Clocktower Mill 1840
7 Healey Royd Mill
8 Danes House Mill
9 Old Hall Mill 1902
a Livingstone Mill 1887
b Barden Mill 1920
c Pendle View Mill
d Brierfield Mill
e Hollin Bank Mill
f Whitefield Mill

where a ground floor workshop is topped by a terrace of two-storey workers' cottages accessed by a balcony incorporating a cast-iron balustrade. Wake at dawn, and all you had to do was go downstairs to work. Cunning devils, the bosses, disguising this arrangement as altruism.

The canal's western entry into Burnley is by way of GANNOW TUNNEL, a towpathless, 559 yards long bore which forces towpath walkers to traverse a potentially bewildering network of motorway underpasses and terraced streets. Lucky you have your Canal Companion with you and the enlargement opposite which reveals all.

Manchester Road climbs up from Burnley's Town Hall and celebrated Mechanics Institute to BURNLEY WHARF with its imposing warehouses and overhanging canopy betraying a family resemblance to Eanam Wharf at Blackburn. If anything, this Burnley example is even more impressive and makes a fitting location for the Weaver's Triangle visitor centre housed in the wharfmaster's house and toll office.

British Waterways maintenance yard and office was moving to Rose Grove as we went to press, leaving the old Finsley Gate dockyard (where generations of short boats and wide boats were built and maintained) mothballed pending the establishment of a marina on the site. With water, refuse and sanitary disposal facilities, FINSLEY GATE WHARF provides essentially the most secure and town-centre handy moorings for boaters visiting Burnley.

Mills, wharves, tunnels: all good clean fun, but Burnley's most astonishing canal gesture, and one of the Seven Wonders of the Waterways, is the embankment which carries the Leeds & Liverpool across the broad, converging valleys of the Calder and Brun, to the east of the town centre. Sixty feet high, and three-quarters of a mile long, BURNLEY EMBANKMENT affords the canal traveller a bird's eye view of the town: a seemingly endless railway viaduct; the bus park with its cream-coloured Burnley & Pendle single-deckers; Turf Moor football stadium where Burnley, a club with a pedigree as proud as Blackburn's down the cut, were fighting (unsuccessfully) to avoid relegation to the Second Division when we passed through; slate rooftops of densely packed terraced streets which gleam dully after a shower like corroded silver; a largely petrified forest of factory chimneys; and all this horizoned by backdrops of wild moorland; an escape clause for all those consigned to an occluded existence in these Pennine textile towns. On one of the tops to the south-east a wind farm gesticulates madly. The embankment was almost our nemesis. Days before our research boat was due to cross it, we learnt from British Waterways that a stoppage for repairs to Yorkshire Street Aqueduct was likely to overrun. Fearing the worst, we put through a telephone call to Lancashire County Council who, to their eternal credit, pulled whatever strings were necessary to enable us to sail across the embankment; while the scaffolding was still in place and almost before the concrete had dried!

North of the embankment the canal skirts a pretty municipal park and crosses an aqueduct carrying it over the River Brun, one of the shortest rivers we can think of, rising on the flanks of Worsthorne Moor, just three or four miles to the east, and colliding with the Calder in some obscure corner of Burnley town centre. The "Burnley Way", a forty mile footpath circling the district, follows the Brun upstream from here. In earlier times a mineral railway serving Bank Hall Colliery passed beneath the aqueduct. The mine's barge loading basin is still in water by the sharp turn in the canal, as is a former drydock nearby. Bank Hall's first shaft was sunk in 1860, but perhaps its busiest period for canal traffic was in the middle of the twentieth century when it was the principal supplier of coal to Whitebirk power station at Blackburn. The pit was finally closed in 1972 on safety grounds following the discovery of excess gases in its galleries.

The canal makes its northern exit from Burnley past a series of handsome textile mills, Livingstone - perhaps the most resplendent - having been adopted by the local authority for use as a training centre. The single-track railway to Colne comes alongside, its services mostly provided by solo railcars. By the railway bridge (132A) the canal widens at the site of Reedley Colliery loading basin, but between here and Brierfield the waterway surfaces for a gulp of fresh air. Good honest countryside intervenes, together with a sense of remoteness heightened by the proximity of so much urbanisation. Pendle Hill (1831ft) looks good from this angle, and the villages cuddled in the folds of its south-facing flank hold memories of the notorious Lancashire Witches. But at BRIERFIELD the mills come back, two of the largest belonging now to Smith & Nephew and engaged in the lucrative business of producing medical gauze.

CATHARSIS comes to the cut. Depending on your direction of travel, you are about to exchange the satanic textile towns of East Lancashire with the wide open spaces of rural Pendle, or vice versa.

NELSON churns down its hillside to the canal bank in a vortex of mills and still-cobbled streets. Your subconscious is disappointed not to come upon George Formby "leaning on a lamppost at the corner of a street", even if these days any "certain little lady" going by is likely to be of Asian descent; though her dialect will remain disarmingly Pennine.

It must be disorientating to live in 19th century streets like these without out of town retail parks just a magic carpet ride down the motorway. But our old friends the industrial archaeologists will be having a field day picking over the finer points of

mill chimney decoration and lost in admiration for the attractively restored three-storey canalside warehouse at Yarnspinner's Wharf by bridge 141A, a brick-built cousin of the structures at Burnley and Blackburn. Bridge 141B is overlooked by Seed Mills where carpet yarn is spun, and, on the towpath side, the engine house of the Pendle Street Power Co dated 1885.

Pendle Hill continues to provide the thematic sub-text to your journey, poking its nose in whenever there's a lapse in industry's small talk. BARROWFORD LOCKS, popular with sightseers, carry the canal some seventy feet up out of the valley of the Colne and Pendle waters to its six mile summit pound, four hundred and eighty-seven feet above sea level. The flight derives its name from the weaving village to the west, whilst the important town of Colne straddles

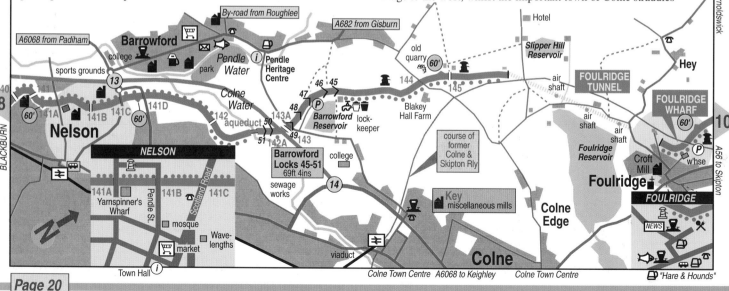

a hillside in the opposite direction, the clocktower of its town hall dominating the view against the moorland backdrop of the Forest of Trawden. Less than ten miles over there lies Haworth and Bronteland.

Back alongside the canal, Barrowford Reservoir receives what excess water the summit might have to offer. A small car park is provided for motorised visitors to the flight. A country mile to the north Blacko Tower overlooks proceedings. It was erected in 1890 by a grocer called Jonathan Stansfield who preferred folies to women and alcohol. He may have had a point.

Pleasant farmland intervenes between Barrowford top lock (where water and refuse disposal facilities are obtainable) and the western portal of Foulridge's celebrated tunnel. The 1,640 yards long tunnel's claim to fame lies not so much in the fact that it is the longest on the Leeds & Liverpool Canal, but that it was the scene, in 1912, of one of the

Barrowford Locks

more bizarre events in the annals of bovine history, when a cow called Buttercup fell into the canal at the western end of the tunnel and swam through to the eastern end before being rescued and revived with brandy. What is perhaps not so well known is that Buttercup's unique swimming action subsequently led to the development of a new stroke called the butter*fly,* and that for many years afterwards she acquired cult status on the local swimming gala circuit.

Towpathless, and confined to one-way working, FOULRIDGE TUNNEL was five long years in the making, the cut & cover technique being applied. Leggers gave way to steam tugs in 1880, which in turn survived until 1937, by which time trade over the top was negligible and largely diesel-powered in any case. Colour-light signals control the entry of boats through the tunnel, turning green for ten minutes on the half-hour at the western end and likewise on the hour at the eastern end. Thirty minutes are allowed for passage through the tunnel. Walkers must make their way over the top, the trackbed of the old Colne & Skipton railway providing a useful footpath, though sticky in places, and after prolonged periods of wet weather the local lanes are probably preferable. FOULRIDGE WHARF is a magnet for the boater and the land-based canal enthusiast alike. A trip boat plys from here, there are tearooms, a well-preserved stone warehouse (with Leeds & Liverpool Carrying Co still perceptible on its gable end) and an unusual trestle railway bridge carrying the course of the Colne & Skipton railway. But in many respects the highlight of the wharf is a restored limekiln erected early in the construction of the canal to provide lime for mortar, which relied initially on Lothersdale limestone brought in by 'lime gals'. Not, to some of our crew's regret, stocky local wenches with descendents in the vicinity, but sturdy Galloway ponies.

*T*HERE really should be some ceremonial equivalent on the Leeds & Liverpool of the crossing of the equator as one passes from Lancashire to Yorkshire; from the land of Gracie Fields to the land of Geoffrey Boycott. Meddlesome politicians arranged for the time honoured boundary to be moved in 1974. Prior to that it crossed the canal between bridges 149 and 150 where a feeder from Whitemoor Reservoir enters the canal overlooked by a big stone mill with attractive employees houses alongside. Barnoldswick apart, with its Rolls Royce plant - where Frank Whittle's dreams of jet propulsion really took off - and Silent Night bed factory housed partially in an old canalside textile mill, the canal's journey is predominantly rustic in character.

Scar tissue from abandoned canal and railway branches can still be discerned. The Rain Hall Rock canal was cut to expedite the extraction of limestone from an aquatic, linear quarry face. In its half mile it included two short tunnels and a viaduct carrying a by-road. Unfortunately, most of its remains have been buried by landfill. 'Barlick' lost its shuttle train service from nearby Earby in 1965. A chunk of the bridge which carried it over the canal remains like a half-eaten apple. The canal shop at Lower Park Marina has the reputation of being the best of its kind in the north.

GREENBERFIELD LOCKS are exquisite and compulsively photogenic. Three single chambers replaced a time-consuming staircase early in the nineteenth century, remains of which can still be seen, including a bridge-hole niftily commandeered as a stable. By the top lock a feeder comes in from Winterburn Reservoir. A picnic site is provided for motorists and use of the towpath boosted by walkers on the "Pendle Way". Greenberfield was to have been the departure point for a branch canal proposed to link the main line with the market town of Settle. The mind boggles with the beauty of what might have been. A dwelling in Settle, now a tea room, bears the name "Liverpool House" in anticipation of the canal which never came. Bridge 156 marks the boundary between the Burnley and Apperley Bridge maintenance sections of British Waterways. To the north the horizon extends to infinity in waves of moorland.

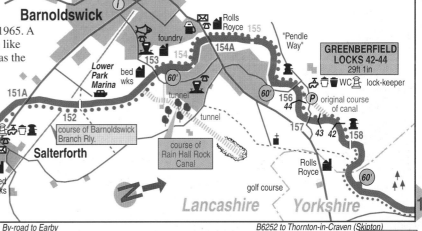

Bancroft Mill mus

Barnoldswick

foundry

Rolls Royce 155

"Pendle Way"

GREENBERFIELD LOCKS 42-44 29ft 1in

WC lock-keeper

Lower Park Marina bed wks

153 154 154A

60'

60' 156 44 original course of canal

tunnel

157 43 42 158

feeder from Whitemoor Res.

151A

mill 150

149

Boat Club

151 152 course of Barnoldswick Branch Rly.

course of Rain Hall Rock Canal

Salterforth

147 148

site of boatbuilding yard

bed wks

sewage plant

tunnel

golf course

Rolls Royce

60'

Lancashire Yorkshire

9

11

B6383 to Kelbrook   By-road to Earby   B6252 to Thornton-in-Craven (Skipton)

THEY say that the only man-made object which astronauts can make out on the earth's surface is the Great Wall of China. But it is difficult to believe that they cannot also see this dizzy, disorientating, peregrinating pool of Marton wriggling and writhing across the upland pastures of the Yorkshire Dales. We enjoyed one of our most idyllic days of boating ever, fine-judging its bindweed bends, a March sun warm on our backs, lapwings and curlews calling overhead, promising a summer which we couldn't make them keep.

This is drumlin country. The propensity of the Ice Age's retreating glaciers to leave their litter behind them has left us with a legacy of profound beauty, for these smooth rounded hillocks are as ravishing as the fleshy contours of the woman in your life. In many respects, Marton Pool is bound to remind seasoned canal travellers of the Oxford Canal's summit; it even has a transmitter mast which seems determined to baffle your sense of direction, and similarly there are apt to moments of confusion when you glimpse what appears to be a boat on another parallel-running canal, only to discover that it is the same canal re-inventing itself time after time.

One could easily be beguiled into mooring up at EAST MARTON forever. All life's essentials are here. A country pub; a cosy cafe serving mouth-watering wedges of coffee-cake; and a traditional red telephone kiosk from which you can call your boss and tell him you've quit. Tempted? But the A59's relentless traffic brings with it a sense of reality and responsibilty, even if the double-arched bridge which carries it is one of the little wonders of the waterways, an engagingly beautiful mother of invention whereby the realigned, upgraded road was simply provided with a second arch above the first. Other travellers enjoy a brief encounter with the canal as the Pennine Way appropriates the towpath for half a mile or so of its 270 mile course from Edale to Kirk Yetholm. Exchange a wave with the back-packers. Your goals may differ but your pace is the same. The journey's the thing in both instances, the intoxication of travel for travel's sake.

BANK NEWTON LOCKS lower the canal helter-skelter down into the valley of the Aire above a sprinkling of typical Dales farmsteads from which the pong of slurry is born bucolically upon the breeze. The locks are notable in retaining clough-type ground paddles by their top gates, a refreshing survival flying in the face of uniformity, and so easy to operate compared with the laborious windings of windlass-operated paddle gear.

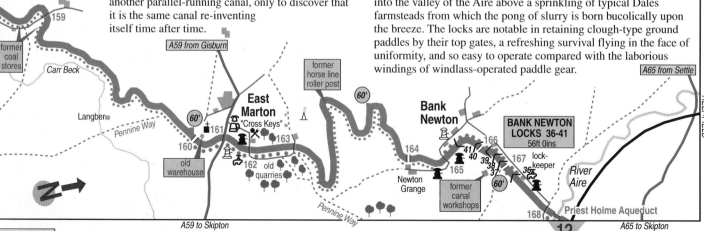

Bank Newton

Marton Pool

MAKING its unfettered way through the deliciously green upper valley of the Aire, the Leeds & Liverpool Canal is overlooked by the russet-coloured crag of Sharp Haw and obelisk-topped Cracoe Fell. GARGRAVE is the only settlement of any significance in what is a surprisingly remote tract of land, especially given the busyness of the A65; West Yorkshire's link with The Lakes. Six locks - almost too dispersed to be considered as a flight - carry the canal through Gargrave, demanding a level of exertion from the boater which can easily be rewarded by a sojourn in this appealing village, for which 3 day visitor moorings are provided above Higher Land Lock.

By bridge 171 an old stone-built warehouse overlooks the canal. One can imagine that it was once stuffed with agricultural produce due to be carried out of the district by barge and coal brought in from the coalfields of East Lancs and West Yorks. Coal is still stocked canalside, in an echo of old trading patterns, but naturally it gets here by lorry now, and no longer from Lancashire or Yorkshire; Silesia more likely.

On the southern outskirts of Gargrave, Johnson & Johnson's large factory manufactures medical and family hygene products. We were told that its location in Gargrave is due to the "clean air." With an 'e' or without?

The old Midland Railway's main line to Scotland shares the Aire's broad valley with the road and the canal. Steam specials sometimes use this route on their way to or from the Settle & Carlisle line. Want to know more? Turn to Pearson's Railway Rides: Leeds, Settle & Carlisle, price £5.95 from all good bookshops!

By-road from Grassington

Demesne of Eshton Hall

Eshton Beck

aqueduct

Holme Bridge

Johnson & Johnson

River Aire

Thorlby

A65 from Harrogate

Travel Lodge

Aireville Park

school

Skipton Town Centre

warehouse
coal wharf

Pennine Way

WC

Gargrave House

Gargrave

site of Roman Villa

A629

SKIPTON

By-road to Carleton

A6069

Bridleway from Bell Busk

A65 from Settle

"Anchor Inn"
garden centre

Pennine Way

HELLIFIELD

Inghey Bridge

course of Skipton & Colne Rly

Earby Beck

viaduct

Locks	
30 Holme Bridge Lock	11ft 4ins
31 Low Warehouse Lock	10ft 4ins
32 Higher Land Lock	8ft 0ins
33 Anchor Lock	9ft 2ins
34 Scarland Lock	8ft 7ins
35 Steg Neck lock	10ft 7ins

N

By-road to Broughton

A56 to Colne

CANALSIDE SKIPTON is famous for its ducks, but not so famous for its dog pooh, though both are there in abundance; the latter despite provision of a dog loo. Perhaps it's not so much the dogs that are dirty here, as their owners. All of which is a shame, because Skipton is indisputably the nicest place to visit on the Leeds & Liverpool Canal. And when we tell you that the best moorings are where wide boats once unloaded gasworks' coal, and that they are overlooked by the bus station, well-travelled canal users must avoid thinking laterally of Banbury, where the effect is altogether more degenerate. Yes, Skipton can be an endearing hiatus in any canal itinerary, and in any case, when the buses are as becoming as Pennine Motors' grey and orange coloured, Plaxton-bodied coaches, you cannot really quibble.

Overlooked by handsome, avuncular mills - one now engaged in churning out greetings cards, one converted into dignified flats - the canal saunters through Skipton in an amiable frame of mind, throwing off an arm which slips mysteriously beneath the ramparts of the castle to a spooky terminus where barges used to load stone. No craft longer than 35ft can turn at the far end, so those with lengthier vessels unable to resist the temptation to explore this backwater, have to return with their tiller between their legs, in undignified reverse. This SPRINGS BRANCH, can also be followed on foot, providing an inspired short cut to Stainforth's Celebrated Pie Establishment, all but straddling the second bridge up.

Skipton's suburbs do not overstay their welcome either. Close to the canal there is much evidence of terraced housing (lent additional poise by being of stone) with back alleys, mostly still laid with cobble setts and strung with washing lines. From swing bridge 176 there is access to the broad, green, breathing space of Aireville Park, with its swimming pool and swings and roundabouts. Bridge 179B carries the old branch lines to Grassington and Ilkley out of the town, the former still used by long trains of Tilcon aggregates wagons in a distant echo of the Springs Branch's stone barges, whilst part of the Ilkley route has been transformed into the Embsay Steam Railway, a delightful little line easily reached from Skipton aboard one of Pennine Motors equally charming buses.

Continued over:

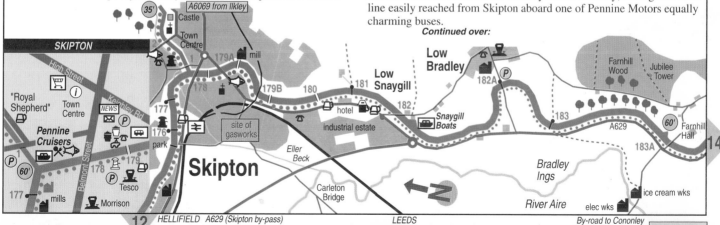

South of Skipton the canal winds prettily through Airedale's lush scenery. Bordered by ings - Yorkshire-speak for ground susceptible to flooding - the Aire meanders along its wide valley which rises to ridges topped by moorland scattered with old quarry workings to the east and lead mines to the west, where one or two smelting chimneys remain to remind us of their worked-out trade. Lockless, constant to the 345ft contour, and interspersed with hand-cuff locked swing bridges - of which BRADLEY BRIDGE (182A) is a particularly obstinate example - the waterway parallels the old Keighley and Kendal turnpike which still retains cast iron mileposts considerably more ornate than the Leeds & Liverpool's. Walkers may find the traffic intrusive, but most boat engines will out-decibel the largest juggernaut, at least as far as the steerer is concerned.

Briefly, the canal veers away from the main road to pay court to an old mill village called Low Bradley, then returns to the road and plunges into Farnhill Wood, a good, old-fashioned sort of arboreal glade made up of beech, birch, alder and sycamore growing sturdily out of a floor of moss and fern. Glimpsed through ivy-clad boles, Cononley's mill chimneys punctuate the valley floor. One of the old mills is occupied by the makers of Yorkshire Dales delicious ice cream. And, yes, we would be grateful for a lifetime's supply in return for this unsolicited publicity. Farnhill Hall dates from the 12th century and has four battlemented towers to keep out marauding Scots. Little did they expect us to creep up on them by canal boat.

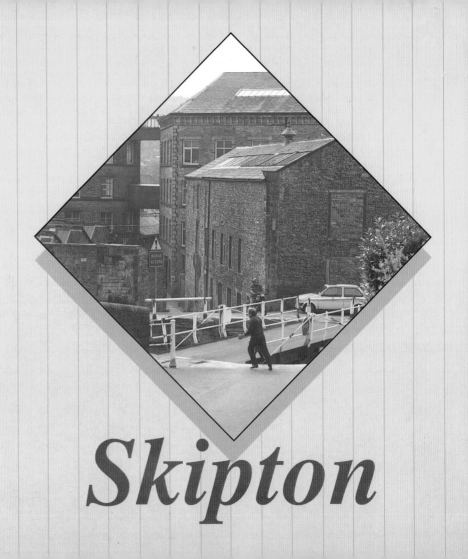

Skipton

CROSSING the boundary between North and West Yorkshire, the Leeds & Liverpool continues its business partnership with Airedale, evoking visions of curly-haired terriers groomed to perfection to show their paces at Crufts. Every pristine dog has its day. Likewise this gorgeous canal, which conjours up one intoxicating view after another. SILSDEN is a handy point for re-stocking the galley from friendly little throw-back shops where you're still expected to reveal your life history over this grocery transaction or that. In the old days Silsden's Co-op's barge, "Progress", worked hard on the canal fetching and carrying produce vital to the little mill town's economy. Nowadays the main street reverberates to juggernauts and the canal wharf has become the point of departure for boating holidaymakers; call that 'progress' if you like.

At the extremities of this map the canal keeps trysts with fauns and nymphs in glades of ancient woodland. Bandying ancient elixirs, they entice you to stay. Certainly there is no excuse for not scrambling up through the bracken and heather

to pay homage to the old queen's - Victoria, that is, not La Rue - Jubilee Tower on Farnhill Moor. Given balmy weather, the view from the top of the Aire Valley, and its lines of communication is invigorating.

Farnhill and Kildwick are cheek by jowl villages separated only by the slender width of the canal. In fact, Kildwick's churchyard has spilt over on to the Farnhill bank, being linked, appropriately enough, by Parson's Bridge. Here, on a mistbound November day, our research party passed beneath the bridge as a funeral cortege carried a coffin overhead towards a black-caped priest and a throng of mourners waiting beside a freshly-dug grave. We were journeying along the longest canal, but it occurred to us that the occupant of that coffin was making - or had perhaps already made - the longest journey of all.

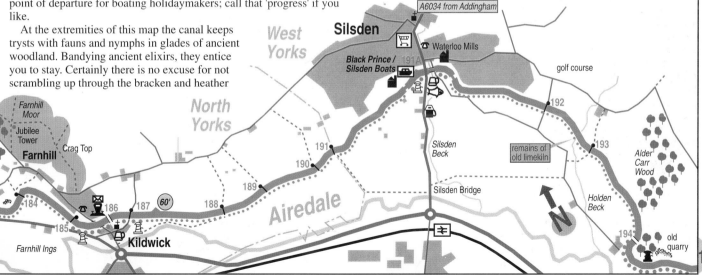

West Yorks

North Yorks

A6034 from Addingham

Silsden

Waterloo Mills

Black Prince / Silsden Boats

191

golf course

192

Farnhill Moor

Jubilee Tower

Crag Top

Farnhill

191

190

189

Silsden Beck

remains of old limekiln

193

Alder Carr Wood

13

184

186

187

60'

188

185

Kildwick

Farnhill Ings

Airedale

Silsden Bridge

Holden Beck

N

194

old quarry

15

Kildwick

HAPPY-GO-LUCKILY lockless, the canal slots snugly into a ledge above the Aire's suddenly constricted valley, blind to all the blandishments that the kerb-crawling town of Keighley can offer to become better acquainted.

Bridges 197A, 198A and 199 are sophisticated, electrically operated swing affairs, for which you will need a BW sanitary key and some experience in the day to day management of a small power station to open. We were unable to extract the key from one of them and had to abandon it, passing down the canal to rumours of half-mile traffic tail-backs and a motorist's whip-round to pay for a contract to be put out on the boat crew responsible. British Waterways were more magnanimous, admitting that the electrified bridges were prone to malfunction, especially early in the season, before they had got, so to speak, into the 'swing' of things.

At Stockbridge substantial warehouses recall an era when canal transport played an effective role in Keighley's economy. Wool and sugar were still being carried over the summit from Liverpool docks to these extensive premises in the early Fifties, an activity rudely interrupted on 17th May 1952 by a massive breach in the canal's bank which all but washed away the local golf course. Luckily, three maintenance men, already investigating a reported leak in the canal, had enough presence of mind to leap clear of the sudden deluge. Even more fortunately, they were able to insert stop planks into narrows built during the second world war in case of bomb damage, so confining the effect of the breach to one instead of seventeen miles.

Of course, in those days - especially 'Up North' - folk made their own entertainment, and the breach was big news. Four policemen were put on special duty to control the excited crowds. People poured in from all over the West Riding almost as rapidly as the water had poured out of the canal. Ten 'expert puddlers' were sent over from Wigan to reline the canal bed. They must have walked straight out of a Monty Python sketch. Ten clones in hobnail boots and braces elbowing their way like gladiators through the hushed throng - "It's t'puddlers!" - and proceeding to go about their routine like a Morris dance in slow motion amidst spontaneous outbursts of applause from a crowd hardly able to contain themselves. Ecky thump!

Scratch the past and see what happens. Like the Leeds & Liverpool itself, the magic is never very far from the surface. Look closely at the corner of the wooden warehouse by bridge 197, and you will find flyboat semaphore signals (tucked away in the down position) which once were used to convey messages to the passing boatmen of non-stop boats during the heyday of traffic over the canal, when Foulridge to Stockbridge was considered a good day's work for a boat horse. In pleasure-boating terms, the mind baulks at coming to terms with such distances.

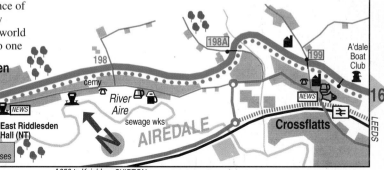

THE civilised world is divided into those who know Bingley as a centre of thermal underwear manufacture, and those who recognise it as the location of one of the Seven Wonders of the Waterways, the gargantuan BINGLEY FIVE RISE staircase locks. You know, of course, where our interests lie. Yes, that's right, just look at the lacework on that plunge neckline, darling!

The Leeds & Liverpool goes in for a fair amount of plunging too. It plunges down the 5 Rise, it plunges down the 3 Rise; and you too can plunge, metaphorically, into the clam chowder-like waters of the West Riding, a landscape as warmfully, playfully hugging as the latest little number from Damart.

But you'll be wanting some facts, and the facts are that the 5 Rise changes the level of the canal by some sixty vertiginous feet, a thrombotic experience which the canal takes more or less in its stride, even if it leaves most canal users reeling. The staircase has stood its ground since 1774 and must be credited to John Longbotham, the L&L's chief engineer.

Two centuries later it's the pride and joy of its resident lock-keeper,

Barry Whitelock, an appropriately surnamed young man who reminds you forcibly of Brian Clough in his pomp at Derby County, and who has a way of treating boat crews and onlookers (of which there are often hundreds at a time) as if they were taking part in one of Cloughie's training sessions all those years ago.

Most of the time Barry will supervise passage through the 5 Rise, working most of the complex paddle gear himself whilst keeping a paternal eye on the proceedings. We hit the locks, however, on the first busy Saturday of the season, and he was called away to assist a wideboat down the 3 Rise, leaving us, effectively, to operate the last four chambers of the 5 Rise for ourselves. It felt a little bit like turning up at the airport and having the pilot ask if we'd mind awfully taxi-ing out on to the runway while he nipped off for a newspaper. It was worth the licence fee. Adrenalin-pumping, we progressed from one cavernous chamber to the next like

Key

1 Miscellaneous mills
2 Damart Works
3 Former sawmill
4 Salts Mills
5 Orbic Works
6 Airedale Mills
7 Junction Mills

Hainsworth's Boatyard

BINGLEY 5 RISE
No.s 25-29
60ft 0ins
lock-keeper

Bingley 3 Rise
No.s 22-24
30ft 0ins

Dowley Gap 2 Rise
No.s 20 & 21
18ft 4ins
lock-keeper

Hirst Lock
No.19 10ft 2ins

Shipley Glen Tramway

River Aire

Bingley
park

Safeway

Saltaire

former canal warehouses

Apollo Cruisers

Shipley

course of Bradford Canal

Moorhead

Waterbus Stops

aqueduct

River Aire

school

Baildon ILKLEY A6038 from Otley

A657 to Leeds

A650 from Keighley SKIPTON

B6429 from Harden

A650 to Bradford   A650 to Keighley   Bradford city centre 3 miles

15   17

200 201 202 203 204 205 206 207 207A 207B 207C 207D 208 209 209A

seasoned bargees, playing to the gallery of assembled onlookers.

Set on a bend overlooked by Damart's huge mill, the 3 Rise is scarcely less intimidating, but by now we were old hands. Between the bottom chamber and bridge 202 the canal has been diverted to accommodate a controversial new road. There is no access from the towpath to the town, but a length of visitor moorings is provided on the off-side by the waterbus stop with access to the road carried over the canal by bridge 202. As at Saltaire and Shipley, Bingley's station is handily alongside, and thus ideal for one-way towpath walks.

Shaking off high-rise suburbs, the canal proceeds through the glacial moraines of Dowley Gap. Bridge 204 carries the pipework of Bradford Corporation's Nidd Aqueduct water supply channel. DOWLEY GAP 2 RISE lies alongside a sizeable sewage works, but the resident lock-keeper turns his back and regularly wins prizes for the loveliness of his locks, and with the "Fisherman's Inn", adjacent to nearby Scourer Bridge (205) this is a pleasant and reputedly secure spot to moor overnight.

A seven-arch aqueduct spans a reach of the Aire used by the rowing fraternity before the canal enjoys a woodland interlude to the north of HIRST LOCK, where there is an interesting little gathering of old mill buildings and associated housing together with another waterbus stop. Operated by Apollo Cruisers of Shipley (01274 595914) on Bank holidays and weekends through the summer, between Shipley and Bingley, the waterbus is a popular feature along this length of canal. Likewise the towpath, a regular haunt of walkers and runners throughout the year.

SALTAIRE holds a unique place on the canal system. Alright, the Worcester & Birmingham skims through Bournville, but there is barely any hint of the model worker's village beyond the towpath, whilst Port Sunlight and New Lanark have no canals at all. And so Saltaire deserves to be savoured, as perhaps Sir Titus always intended: its canyon of fudge-coloured mills, elegant Congregational church and streets of dignified worker's housing named after Titus Salt's children. Moor here, or detour from the towpath, and stroll across the Aire to the Shipley Glen Tramway, a weird Victorian cable incline conveying open carriages up and down through a wooded hillside.

Unlike Saltaire, SHIPLEY has few pretentions to architectural style, though its massive canal warehouses create a distinct impression by virtue of their size alone. Once they would have been stuffed to the gills with angora fleeces. Now they are being refurbished. Their simple dignity contrasts with futuristic office blocks strung along the opposite bank of the canal. Architecture oscillating between the centuries. But it's 'no contest' really, and it takes the unselfconscious functionalism of PACE's premises by swing bridge 209 (hand-cranked by windlass) to provide a favourable effect at the end of the 20th century. Junction Mills recall the former egress, by bridge 208, of the Bradford Canal, once described as "a seething cauldron of impurity." It was apparently so polluted by the waste from mills and dyeworks as to burn with a blue gas flame. It was abandoned in 1922. Shipley railway station has an unusual triangular layout, though its handsome Midland Railway signal boxes have been removed following electrification of the Airedale lines between Leeds and Skipton, Bradford and Ilkley.

Dowley Gap

EACH succeeding era of transport has more effrontery than the last. The new Airedale relief road blitzkriegs its way through Bingley impervious to the finer feelings of anything in its path. Similarly, the railway builders of the mid nineteenth century had no qualms about tunnelling under The Nosegay. But the hesitant 18th century canal builders, aware of their engineering inexperience, chose to follow the Aire Valley. Their hesitancy is our gain, for the canal's course is prettily wooded and not at all compromised by the proximity of Bradford Corporation's huge sewage works at Esholt, so extensive that it once boasted its own network of railway lines shunted with steam locomotives fuelled by the waste oils from wool. By swing bridge 211B the main part of the works - imposingly built in hefty stone with liberal scrollwork and coats of arms - was served by a barge basin which remains in water, if not in use;

though barges were still carrying effluent from Esholt to Knostrop, south of Leeds, at the beginning of the Eighties. A high security fence protects the plant from the attentions of sewage enthusiasts, who might otherwise force an entry and make off with lumps of the stuff as souvenirs. Not readily visible from the canal, Esholt village doubles as "Emmerdale", Yorkshire Television's soap opera of everyday farming folk.

DOBSON LOCKS, a 2 Rise, lie alongside British Waterways' manager's office and maintenance yard. Strange to think that all those miles of canal between Greenberfield and Leeds are overseen from this modest collection of workshops and canal worker's cottages. It is no secret, however, that British Waterways derive much of their present income from property deals, a facet of their business demonstrated by the new "Moorings" development at Apperley Bridge. The stone built houses, congregating around a newly dug basin, are pleasing to the eye and harmonise well with the adjoining textile mill erected in 1896.

The canal curves endearingly around the perimeter of Calverley Wood where old quarry faces once provided work for barges. Woodhouse Grove School's playing fields run down to the banks of the Aire. Here, on a bleary winter's afternoon in 1969, your hero scored a scintillating try from a five yard tap penalty.

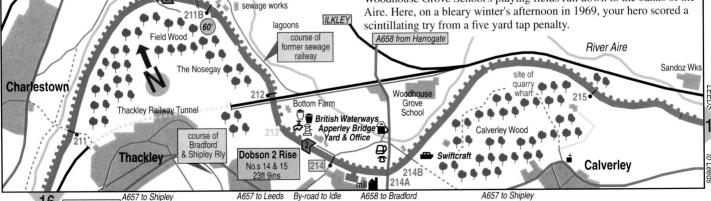

ILKLEY A6038 from Otley

By-road from Esholt (aka "Emmerdale")

Field 3 Rise No.s 16-18 25ft 0ins

3

211B

60'

Field Wood

The Nosegay

N

Charlestown

Thackley Railway Tunnel

211

Thackley

course of Bradford & Shipley Rly

Dobson 2 Rise No.s 14 & 15 23ft 9ins

214

River Aire sewage works

lagoons

course of former sewage railway

212

Bottom Farm

213

British Waterways Apperley Bridge Yard & Office

2

214A 214B

mill

ILKLEY

A658 from Harrogate

River Aire

Sandoz Wks

Woodhouse Grove School

site of quarry wharf

215

Calverley Wood

Swiftcraft

Calverley

LEEDS Abs/ to Leeds

SHIPLEY

REMINDING one more of the Worcester & Birmingham's approach to Birmingham than the Bridgewater's entrance into Manchester, the Leeds & Liverpool Canal wears its green heart on its sleeve as it winds through the leafy suburbs of Rodley, Newlay and Kirkstall. The canal builders had no ambitions beyond following the Aire. Perhaps, had it not been so mercurial a watercourse, they might have considered making it navigable. But after a day or two of rain in the Dales, the river's current sweeps all before it, illustrating exactly why it would have been pretty much impractical to use it as the basis of a navigation. The suburbs are 19th and 20th century phenomenons. In the 18th century Airedale was a virtual arcady. Artists as famous as Turner were attracted by its romantic melancholy, especially Kirkstall Abbey. Turner painted Kirkstall Lock in 1824. British Waterway's last painted it in 1982. Despite the prevalance of so much greenery, there are outbreaks of industry worth looking out for. A crane-making works was

established at RODLEY in 1820. Here they built plant for some of the world's most prestgious civil engineering projects, from the Aswan Dam to the Manchester Ship Canal. Aire Vale Dyeworks date from 1877, whilst by bridge 222, the former Kirkstall Brewery has been converted to provide accommodation for Leeds Metropolitan University students. At one time the canal played an important role in transporting the brewery's output. Hogheads of beer were taken by barge to Goole and transhipped for export on to the brewery's own steamships which traded as far afield as the Antipodes. Nowadays the trade is reversed, and we must put up with "Castlemaine XXXX". But perhaps the most significant industrial activity in this part of the Aire Valley is Kirkstall Forge, where the drop-hammers still thump through each working day as they have done since the 17th century. Nowadays the forge belongs to GKN and specialises in the production of axles for road vehicles.

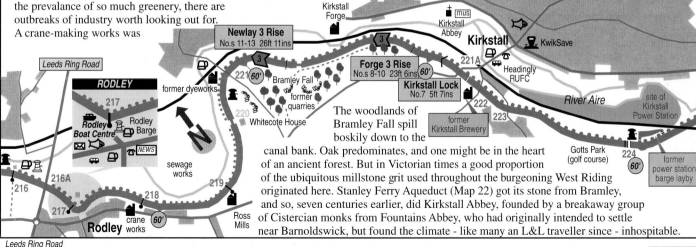

The woodlands of Bramley Fall spill boskily down to the canal bank. Oak predominates, and one might be in the heart of an ancient forest. But in Victorian times a good proportion of the ubiquitous millstone grit used throughout the burgeoning West Riding originated here. Stanley Ferry Aqueduct (Map 22) got its stone from Bramley, and so, seven centuries earlier, did Kirkstall Abbey, founded by a breakaway group of Cistercian monks from Fountains Abbey, who had originally intended to settle near Barnoldswick, but found the climate - like many an L&L traveller since - inhospitable.

LEEDS, a milestone in any journey: whether it be the last, northern rites of the M1, a hiatus of concrete amongst the terraced houses and lock-up workshops of Holbeck; as a launch pad for the majestic Midland Railway's line to Scotland, alias the Settle & Carlisle; or, in this case, a change of gauge, on what could be a 'Voyage Between Two Seas.' When Pete Morgan arrived here in 1982, on film his so-named journey from the Mersey to the mouth of the Humber for a much-loved BBC television series, he met with Joe Bridge, holder of the unofficial 'Blue Riband' for the canal journey from Liverpool to Leeds. In 1944 he had skippered a horse-drawn cargo of sugar from Tate & Lyle's Liverpool works to Leeds Basin in 52 hours.

Most traffic in the canal was less long distance in character. The major user at this end was Leeds Corporation's Electricity Department who opened a spanking new power station at Kirkstall in 1931 and fed its furnaces with coal brought in by convoys of barges from the Wakefield and Castleford coalfields. Electricity was also generated at a city centre plant on Whitehall Road, which barges reached through a now vanished lock down into the Aire located in the bowels of City railway station. Nowadays, these bowels, or "Dark Arches", liberally doused with Epsom Salts, look very well indeed, having been transformed from gloomy catacombs into the "Granary Wharf", a centre for specialist craft shops and small businesses. But in some respects Leeds lags behind the likes of Manchester and Birmingham in the revitalisation of its canal basin, seemingly content to use it as a car park, though refurbishment of the fine stone warehouse alongside River Lock - the formal boundary between the Leeds & Liverpool Canal and the Aire Navigation - as a restaurant and offices, will hopefully have a knock-on effect. Surely the basin could realise more income for its owners as a prime site for property speculation, than as a £3.50 a day car park.

Travelling into, or out of, Leeds by canal exposes one to a succulent slice of the city's industrial heritage, the history of which is neatly encapsulated by the displays and artefacts

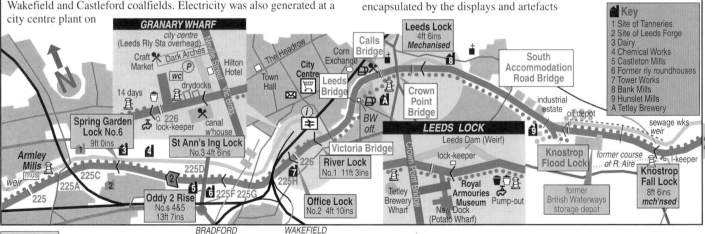

Key
1 Site of Tanneries
2 Site of Leeds Forge
3 Dairy
4 Chemical Works
5 Castleton Mills
6 Former rly roundhouses
7 Tower Works
8 Bank Mills
9 Hunslet Mills
A Tetley Brewery

splendidly housed within the museum at ARMLEY MILLS. Here you can learn how the L&L played a significant role in the transformation of Leeds from a modest wool town into England's third largest city, then step outside on to the towpath and encounter a good many of the cast of that metamorphosis in the flesh, or rather in brick and mortar and millstone grit. Highlights of the journey between Armley Mills and River Lock include: the viaduct which carries the Harrogate line over the Aire Valley at bridge 225C; the sites of Leeds Forge (which once built high pressure boilers for the Royal Navy and rolling stock underframes for the Empire's railway systems) and Leeds's formerly intensive tanning industry; the handsome Castleton Mill built in 1838 for the weaving of flax; the Leeds & Thirsk Railway's round-houses by bridge 225D; and the extraordinary Tower Works looming over OFFICE LOCK, its chimneys heavily disguised as campaniles. Inside, the workforce were not, as you might expect, busily churning out operatic arias, but engaged in the slightly more mundane pastime of manufacturing pins and combs for the wool trade. Those Victorians and their architectural hang-ups! Moor here overnight and you are apt to wake up drowsily imagining that you've floated on to Florence or Verona, until the rumble of the seven-twelve to Huddersfield brings you back to the West Riding with a bump.

The Aire & Calder Navigation

If Granary Wharf lacks a little revivalist zeal, the city's riverfront makes bounteous amends. If there is a more fascinating, adrenalin-pumping urban navigation in the country - Westminster and the Thames notwithstanding - it does not spring readily to mind. We may have been bowled over by the crisp autumnal light illuminating the old warehouses and their modern imposters on the day we made our initial reconnaissance for this guide. And yes, alright, under a sullen Pennine sky it may look all somewhat less prepossessing. But first impressions of places, like people, are difficult to shake off. VICTORIA BRIDGE was designed by George Leather jnr, the Aire & Calder's engineer. Opened in 1839, it replaced an earlier structure swept away by floodwaters. The current can still be capricious, and

boaters are advised not to pass down through River Lock if the gauge at the tail of the lock shows only red. Go and watch the current coursing through the Dark Arches and you will see how volatile the Aire can be. But it was made navigable up to Leeds as early as 1700, bringing in its wake, a camp following of mills, warehouses and wharves, so intimate with each other as to create an orgy of industrial premises with the river winding through it. Old engravings, oil paintings and photographs reveal a waterway crowded with vessels like any ring-road at rush hour. Though unlike any ring-road at rush hour, the effect is visually satisfying, even if the river was, by all accounts horribly polluted in the heyday of the water trade. The riverside buildings span the centuries, from 19th century brick warehouses to the futuristic glass and concrete of Tetley's Brewery Wharf. Where refurbishment has not been practical, new buildings, like the ASDA supermarket chain's head office, have been erected in pleasing harmony.

LEEDS BRIDGE dates from 1873, though there had been a succession of earlier structures at this point since the original ferry was replaced late in the 14th century. It was cast at Butlers Ironworks, Stanningley and has a span of 102ft 6ins. On the south bank, east of the bridge, stand the remnants of the Aire & Calder Navigation's once extensive warehouses which included a covered dock now partially retained as a water feature for a development of modern housing. The company's palatial offices fronting the corner of Dock Street remain in use by British Waterways as regional headquarters. But it is the presently empty building adjoining the bridge which has the most interesting story - or rather, two stories - to tell. Two plaques above the parapet reveal that the teetotal Band of Hope was founded in this building in 1847, and that the first moving pictures taken with a

One or two sections of towpath are absent between Granary Wharf and Crown Point Bridge. Follow the blue dots indicated on the map between Victoria Bridge via Leeds Bridge and Dock Road to Calls Bridge.

single lens camera were made from an upstairs window by Louis le Prince forty-one years later. Magic, or what?

Downstream, you float down the Aire under the gothic gaze of Leeds Parish Church and the mordant wit of yuppies on wine bar balconies to CALLS BRIDGE, a modern footbridge opened in 1993 to improve access between either bank of the revitalised river. The opportunity to moor is here, as long as you remember to leave sufficient slack for any change which might occur in the river level while you're away. We left the boat, walked with the spirits of long departed boatmen along still-cobbled Dock Street, and lunched at "The Adelphi" amidst flamboyant Edwardian decor that the Aire & Calder's directors may well have been familiar with.

Tetley's Brewery Wharf occupies the old Corporation Cleansing Department yard, whilst the company's huge brewery can be glimpsed to the rear. CROWN POINT BRIDGE, erected in 1842 to the designs of the Leathers, father and son, was being widened as we went to press. Immediately downstream of the bridge the navigation channel proceeds through an artificial cut avoiding the large weir at Leeds Dam. The cut also provides access to New (or Clarence) Dock, nicknamed 'Tattie Dock' by working boatmen due to the preponderance of potato cargoes. Now this sizeable dock is being incorporated in the prestigious Royal Armouries Museum development, opening Spring 1996.

LEEDS LOCK is now mechanised and in VHF radio contact with River Lock. Between here and Knostrop Flood Lock the Aire, passing under the SOUTH ACCOMMODATION ROAD girder bridge, encounters a degree of uninspiring industrial clutter. The towpath is being developed as part of the Trans Pennine Trail. Hunslet Mills, stand gloomily derelict, though protected as a listed building. It was built in 1838 as a flax mill, but in latter years was used for the manufacture of blankets. More positively, the adjacent wharf is used by barges delivering aggregates and other building materials; the highest upstream point on the Aire & Calder now used by commercial traffic. The Aire splits into three channels: the westernmost arm being the river's original course, now foreshortened and used as an arm for laid-up commercial craft. Two old ladies, which must have been skittish fillies in their day, "Lady Kerr" and "Gladys Lillian", were rusting away when we passed.

The eastern channel was cut at the turn of the century to by-pass the old river, whilst, disconcertingly narrow, the centre route is the navigable one, squeezing through the paired gates of KNOSTROP FLOOD LOCK; not really a 'lock' at all, but a pair of mitred gates left open unless there is heavy flooding. South of the floodgates, British Waterways 1958 freight depot, designed to speed up the transit of goods between water and road, has metaphorically turned its back on the navigation, as if saying: "Bollards to barges."

At KNOSTROP FALL LOCK old piers are all that survive of the gargantuan Hunslet Railway swingbridge erected, late in the 19th century, to carry goods trains around the edge of the city at a time when consideration was being given to conversion of the Aire & Calder into a ship canal capable of handling tall-masted sea-going vessels. Local lore has it that the bridge swung only once - on the day it was tested! Decent moorings are available here (in the inlet at the tail of the lock) on the city's outskirts with a lock-keeper in residence.

Thwaite Mills

INDUSTRY has raped and ransacked the Aire Valley's landscape south-east of Leeds. But what do you expect, wasn't the A&C asking for it? The sadness is, that it all couldn't be done with the dignity of Thwaite Mills, as opposed to the smash & grab techniques of opencast mining. For throughout much of this section the countryside resembles a First World War battlefield. Airedale transmogrified into Paschendale. Though like all battlefields after the battle it is haunted by a strange tranquillity, a genius loci of lost causes and pyrrhic victories.

The Aire was powering a fulling mill at Thwaite in the 17th century, but the gorgeous grouping of almost orange brick buildings, apparently haphazardly laid out upon the isthmus between the canal and river now, date from the first quarter of the 19th century. Down the years the mill has crushed seed to make oil, ground flint for pottery, and chalk to turn into putty. Then, following an enforced retirement brought about by flood damage in 1976, it became a working museum. Skelton Grange Power Station looks like another casualty of the 'rush for gas', and no longer hungry for coal brought in by barge (you can still see the lay-by where discharging took place) or railway wagon (two concrete bowspring bridges survive where the trackbed crosses the navigation and the river).

On the far side of this ravaged valley, the massive Tudor-Jacobean facade of Temple Newsam Hall attempts, phlegmatically, to ignore the damage eked out on this once serene landscape, whilst FISHPOND LOCK flippantly evokes a level of monastic charm with which reality can no longer equate. Isolated between latent banks of mining spoil, the lock-keeper's only link with the outside world was a miry track connected umbilically with the former mining village of John O' Gaunts.

There are long stay moorings at WOODLESFORD LOCK, picnic tables and a bird hide overlooking the Aire and adjoining mining flashes. Visitor Moorings are provided by Swillington Bridge. Bentley's Yorkshire Brewery used to stand between the canal and the railway, until it fell into the acquisitive hands of Whitbread who, true to their track record, shut it down. Alcoholic beverage making survives in the district, however, in the somewhat unlikely guise of what is claimed to be England's most northerly commercial vineyard, located across the Aire at Leventhorpe.

At FLEET BRIDGE there used to be a lock down into the Aire. It was retained so that barges could reach Fleet Mills, long ago demolished. And now even the oil staithe, until quite recently served by oil tanker barges, seems forlornly disused.

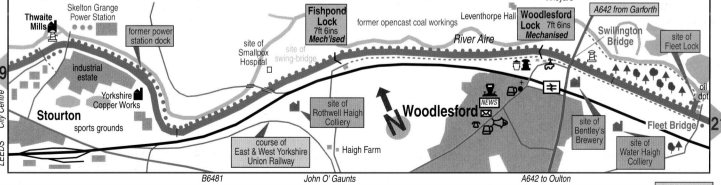

PENNINE

Gauxholme

WATERS

Copley

Page 41

WHY are Castleford's maidens so fair? Because they bathe in the Calder and dry in the Aire. Charming but misrepresentative doggerel: for when we got to the confluence of the Calder with the Aire, there were no bathing beauties, only a chemical plant and a set of traffic lights governing movements to and from the main line of the Aire & Calder Navigation and its Wakefield Branch. But fortune still favours the lasses in this benighted corner of Yorkshire, because the week of our first reccy one of them won the National Lottery.

CASTLEFORD

Lock Lane

NEWS

site of colliery

Allerton Bywater

NEWS

BW

WC

lock-keeper

former coal staithe "The Boat"

Ledston Ings

Aire & Calder to Goole

River Aire

Bulholme Lock
8ft 3ins
Mechanised

chem. wks.
site of former lock

Cawood-Hargreaves

River Aire

site of Kippax Lock

St Aidan's Opencast Mine

opencast coal staithe

Traffic Lights

Castleford Flood Lock
WEIR!

Castleford Bridge

Allinsons Flour Mill
Town Centre

Castleford

chemical works

"The Island"

Coney Moor

Mickletown

Methley Mires

site of glass bottle wks

site of Mere Brewery

footbridge

site of Lemonroyd Old Lock

gravel pit

River Calder

Between Woodlesford and Castleford the Aire has changed its course almost as often as the "Starship Enterprise", most recently in the wake of a massive breach which flooded the adjoining opencast coal workings. So valuable is the coal, however, that British Coal - as one of its last pre-privatisation gestures - footed the £20 million bill for a new alignment to be dug combining the river and canal into one navigable channel

20

LEEDS

Lemonroyd Lock 13ft 6ins
Mechanised

A639 from Leeds

footbridge

l.c.

site of Savile Coly Basin

Methley Bridge

NEWS

Methley

Methley Junction

sewage wks

viaduct

Stephenson's Bridge

22

B6135

WAKEFIELD

between Fleet and Kippax. Built by McAlpines, who apparently approached the job as though they were building a motorway, then simply filled it with water, the new line snakes between raw banks of magnesium-coloured stone and negotiates a deep new lock at Lemonroyd. Engineered on a European scale, you could be making your way between the Rhine and the Danube. Certainly it has been a project, we realised, slightly beyond the scope of our old chums the ten expert puddlers from Wigan.

Provision of a spanking new staithe at St Aidans suggests that some of the opencast coal will be leaving the area by water, but, sadly, upstream of Lemonroyd, commercial activity is confined to Branford's aggregates traffic to Hunslet and the effluent barges that shuttle between Knostrop and Goole, where their cargoes of sewage are transhipped into larger vessels for dumping out at sea.

Allerton Bywater Colliery was the last deep mine in the district. It closed in March 1992. 'Tom Puddings' (tug-hauled compartment boats exclusive to the Aire & Calder - see also Map 22) loaded coal here for export from Goole where each compartment was levitated by means of a massive coal hoist and its contents tipped into the holds of sea-going colliers. This, in the days when Britain was an exporter, rather than an importer, of coal. Two huge, corrugated-iron clad loading shutes stood waterside where now only some masonry banking remains, and the only vessels likely to tie-up here are pleasure craft whose occupants fancy a quiet pint at "The Boat".

CASTLEFORD has always been a waterway crossroads. The Flood Lock is usually open unless there are excess currents in the rivers, and if, as a boater, you intend to stop-over in Castleford, you should pass through the Flood Lock to the Visitor Moorings beyond. East of Castleford the Aire & Calder proceeds through Knottingley (where there is a junction with a navigable section of the River Aire leading to the Selby Canal) to Goole and the tidal Ouse. There is also a connection, by way of the New Junction Canal, with the South Yorkshire Navigation to Sheffield.

But in this guide, we're heading west out of Castleford along the Aire & Calder's Wakefield Branch to join the Calder & Hebble. Between Castleford and Woodnock (Map 22) the navigation traverses a flat landscape occluded by high banks in a manner reminiscent of The Fens. 'Caz' lies hunched across the horizon like someone slumped over a bar. Power lines festoon the fields, glassily reflected in isolated oxbow meanders of the Calder's old course. One of these remained navigable for many years to reach a bottle factory, brewery and pottery works. In the rheumy distance, Ferrybridge's cooling towers foam at the mouth, whilst beyond Allerton Bywater the gracious facade of Ledston Hall reminds one that there was a degree of pre-industrial grace in the vicinity.

Castleford Flood Lock

Though the towpath has been reinstated on the west bank of the Aire, it does not proceed south of Allerton Bywater and through walkers must resort to local lanes via Methley Bridge to rejoin the Calder.

BLACK fades to green as abandoned coal workings are reclaimed, returning Caldervale to its pastoral origins; though there are still eyesores, Fairies Hill having become a landfill site, its sprites turned into seagulls.

When the Castleford & Wakefield Cut was opened in 1839 it almost halved the distance by water between the two towns. Much junketing took place at STANLEY FERRY where the old, sinuous course of the Calder was spanned by an elegant aqueduct, an iron trough suspended between bow-spring girders with classical ornamentations at either end; an elopement of 19th century England with Ancient Greece which is said to have spawned the Sydney Harbour Bridge. Had the aqueduct been in Warwickshire or Northamptonshire or some such county where canals have achieved cult status, it would have been better known. No one paid the structure much attention until British Waterways decided to retire it, by-passing it with a concrete aqueduct itself the victim of a charisma by-pass. Side by side they look like Demi Moore turning up for a premier escorted by Richard Branson. The old aqueduct, they said, wasn't up to taking the strain of modern commercial traffic. But, as is so often the ironic way of things, hardly had the new aqueduct opened when trade all but vanished.

Three automated locks illuminate the boater's progress east of Stanley Ferry. The keeper's days are numbered. When we passed through, the chambers were being made suitable for boater operation, and it seemed that they were about to lose both their homes and their livelihoods; push-buttoned into the past tense by bottom line accountancy; though one or two are to be retained as 'flying' keepers to oversee the occasional passage of commercial

Kirkthorpe

The Half Moon

site of former lock

weir

Broadreach Flood Lock

Harrison's Bridge

site of Park Hill Colliery

Welbeck Land Reclamation Site

course of min rly

CASTLEFORD

Ramsden's Swing Bridge aqueducts

site of West Riding & Silkstone Collieries

M62 Eastbound

WAKEFIELD

old coly basin

Fairies Hill Lock

viaduct

viaduct

site of Altofts Lock

By-road from Altofts (pub, shop, fish & chips)

Birkwood Farm

21

STANLEY FERRY

new aq.

KINGS ROAD LOCK 7ft 0ins *Mechanised*

Birkwood Lock 7ft 0ins *Mechanised*

Ferry Boat Inn

Woodnock Lock 13ft 6ins *Mechanised*

Pennbank Farm

weir

site of Foxholes Lock

site of Bottomboat staithe

River Calder

old aq.

BW

Ship Inn

Lake Lock former A&C maint yrd

course of LMS & LNER Joint Rly

M62 Westbound

A642 to Garforth

craft. Quite apart from the complexity of the new boater-operated, push-button controls, the keepers will be missed. One valued their good humour, their good sense, and the way they called you 'cock' with an easy familiarity suggesting that you were just about to go whippet-racing together. Their canal traverses a lonely, inaccessible, surprisingly agricultural tract of land. Pylons plod across the fields emphasising the efficacy of cramming one's portfolio with electricity shares, just as in the past it paid dividends to invest in the Aire & Calder who, faced with the onset of railway competition, kept abreast of engineering progress by constructing 'cuts' to shorten the river's meanderings, and gradually increasing the dimensions of the locks to accept ever larger craft. Fairies Hill and Altofts locks were by-passed by a new lock at WOODNOCK.

The navigation's old line, spanned by a particularly handsome railway viaduct, provides moorings at either end. But despite such improvements, old reaches of the river continued to be navigated where access was still required to established premises. Foxholes Lock facilitated entry to the Aire & Calder Company's extensive workshops at Stanley. Converted into housing these days, they are still visible on the riverbank beneath the village's impressive church. When the old yard closed, new workshops were opened on the site of a former boatbuilding yard at STANLEY FERRY, and for many years this became a maintenance centre for the 'Tom Puddings', the tug-hauled compartment pans invented by William Hammond Bartholomew,

the A&C's most illustrious manager, for carrying coal. One of the 'Pudding's' regular sources of coal was from St John's Colliery whose basin lay opposite the yard. At one time the compartments were hoisted individually out of the water and conveyed along a mineral railway for loading at the pit head. Nowadays the yard's main activity is the manufacture of lock gates.

South of Stanley Ferry, the canal runs straight through a shallow cutting, site of the 1992 IWA National Waterways Festival. A decade earlier it would hardly have been practical to hold a boat rally here, because this was the location of Park Hill Colliery and a busy loading staithe abutted the canal. Our old friend, Skipton Gas Works, took its coal from here, as did Kirkstall Power Station. Despondency sets it when one contemplates the decline of commercial traffic on the West Riding's waterways; though that has more to do with the retrenchment of heavy industry than any inherent failing in water as a transport mode. We consoled ourselves with slabs of Wendy's celestial fruitcake and the sheer intoxication of boating down a wide waterway under a wide, egg-shell blue sky, imagining ourselves in the wheelhouse of a Humber bound keel (called, perhaps, "Futility") laden with goux destined for the rhubarb fields of the East Riding.

Stanley Ferry

Follow field-path south of Broadreach Flood Lock to/from Map 23. Also note that t/p uses old line of cut at Fairies Hill.

WAKEFIELD marks the boundary between the Aire & Calder and Calder & Hebble navigations, the actual point of demarcation being FALL ING LOCK. East of here the A&C, criss-crossed by railway lines and curves, otherwise unremarkably, around the periphery of the city, passing the barely detectable, and long defunct, junction of the Barnsley Canal. Officially abandoned in 1953, the canal had enjoyed its best years under the ownership of the Aire & Calder when it was a busy outlet for coal from the many pits in the area. At one time it connected with the Sheffield & South Yorkshire Navigation via the Dearne & Dove Canal, a lost route through the swarthy interior of Barnsley's coalfield, intermittently mourned sufficiently enough for restoration to rear its dubious head. Heath Old Hall looms romantically through the treetops on a wooded bluff above the riverbank. Mooring is problematical, but walkers can find their way easily enough up on to the neighbouring common, a delightful throwback to pre-industrial Caldervale.

The Aire & Calder's Wakefield terminus lay adjacent to the city's famous chantry bridge chapel, one of only four remaining in Britain, the others being at Rotherham, Bradford-on-Avon and the Cambridgeshire St Ives, tempting one to devise an inland waterway itinerary visiting all four bridge chapels by boat. Some fascinating old warehouses and offices remain intact around the Aire & Calder's basin but the arm itself is no longer navigable.

A short length of cut - providing useful mooring facilities for Wakefield - separates Fall Ing and Wakefield Flood locks. The latter provides access to (and egress from) a broad reach of the Calder

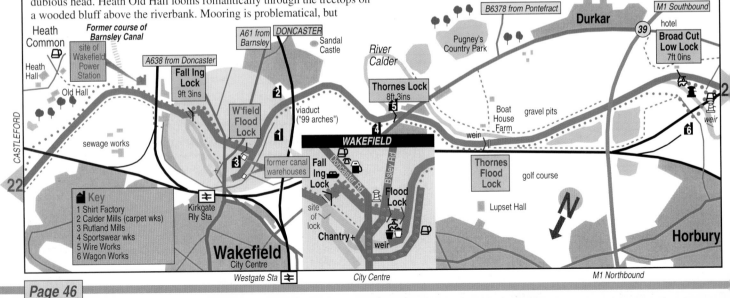

Key
1. Shirt Factory
2. Calder Mills (carpet wks)
3. Rutland Mills
4. Sportswear wks
5. Wire Works
6. Wagon Works

Fall Ing Lock

overlooked by some interesting mills and warehouses. Trade here must have been brisk. Boat captains were apparently in the habit of speculating in local property as an investment towards retirement. Two notable riverside industries still in business are the Wakefield Shirt Company (Double Two) and Rawsons Carpets which was still receiving consignments of jute and coir fibre by barge in the mid Seventies. Nearby, modern double-deckers occupy garaging facilities once devoted to the upkeep of Wakefield's trams.

The main railway route between London and Leeds crosses the Calder upon a cast iron bridge (with battlemented abutments) incorporated into a lengthy viaduct. Locally this is known as the "ninety-nine arches", though some myth-shattering guidebooks would have it that there are only ninety-five. Have they no soul? There are glimpses, upstream, of the motte & bailey remains of Sandal Castle, whilst nearby a housing estate occupies the site of the Battle of Wakefield in 1460, one of the rainbow-coloured reminders that "Richard of York gave battle in vain." The north bank of the river is given over to vegetable growing against a backdrop of Wakefield's skyline, dominated by the soaring spire of the city's cathedral and the high clock-towered town hall.

Thornes Cut eradicates a discursive meander. Once upon a time THORNES LOCK had duplicated chambers. The adjoining wire works has a large asbestos clad warehouse with a canopy overhanging the river, suggesting that water transport was favoured in the past.

Between THORNES FLOOD LOCK and BROAD CUT LOW LOCK the Calder runs through an area of gravel working and passes beneath the M1 motorway. Elmley Moor's massive transmitting mast - taller than the Eiffel Tower - is a dominant landmark to the south-west. In the old days a ferry carried the boat horses across the Calder at Broad Cut Low Lock. Now walkers are faced with a detour by way of the nearby railway bridge, somewhat un-nervingly provided with a pitch-black walkway sandwiched between the tracks above and the foaming waters of the river below. Excuse enough, were any needed, for a fortifying pint of 'Landlord' and a 'Hector Ellis' pie at the neighbouring "Navigation".

Calder Grove

RUNNING to the south of the town of HORBURY, along a five mile section of man-made cut, the Calder & Hebble conveys a surprising sense of isolation, a feeling intensified by the cessation of coal mining in the area. Opening of the cut, piecemeal, eradicated some of the Calder's most extravagant meanderings and lessened delays caused by flooding; though, as we have noted elsewhere, as several industries were already established along the riverbank, some sections of navigation were retained and locks provided through from the new cut to the river. Examples of this are to be seen at HORBURY BRIDGE - where the old connecting basin has been redeveloped as moorings - and at FIGURE OF THREE LOCKS where the abandoned chamber now acts as an overflow weir. The Calder itself has also seen changes to its course, some natural, others, like its realignment to facilitate the construction of Healey Mills marshalling yard, man made. It was the original shape of the river at Healey which gave the locks their unusual name.

Between BROAD CUT TOP LOCK and bridge 32 the canal traverses a melancholy girder-spanned, heron-haunted corridor of silver birch and cindery wasteground climaxed by the death knell ruin of the British Oak Colliery loading staithe, last used in 1981. Oh to see again a West Country keel (no clottted cream connotation, but rather the vessels which gravitated towards the west of the Humber's working waterways) chugging up the cut laden with coal from British Oak destined for Thornhill Power Station on the far side of Dewsbury. Oh to be in England when it did an honest day's work and was not simply content to be a virtual reality, modem-linked annex of Disneyland.

Virgin fields blanket the site of Hartley Bank Colliery. Some of the bridges retain charming triangular Calder & Hebble number plates. Half urban, half rural, the canal reminded us of the lower echelons of the Caldon Canal where it tries to shake off the shackles of The Potteries. It is at Figure of Three that westbound travellers encounter their first example of the Calder & Hebble's indigenous handspike-worked paddle gear. An initiation ceremony ensues. Men are separated from boys; engineers from poets.

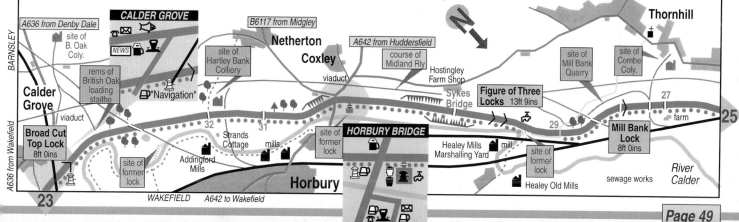

THE deeper the Calder & Hebble journeys up its valley, the more colloquial it becomes. You can almost picture, in all those stern of countenance, millstone grit villas, so many 'Nora Battys' masticating lemon bonbons and washing out the wrinkles in their support stockings. The Calder & Hebble could do with ironing-out its own wrinkles, needing all the support it can get, for in the Thornhill Cut, together with the river section downstream of Greenwood, it is at its least edifying. Usually only too susceptible to the neo-romantic siren call of post-industrial decay, even we felt disenfranchised by the sheer ugliness of these waters, deeming this stretch as vile as any we had ever come upon on our canal travels; BCN nothwithstanding. But perhaps we were tired, or depressed by the weather, or furious with the brambles on the overgrown towpath, or cheated by the absence of orange-coloured Hargreaves

keels plying to and from the now obliterated power station wharf at Thornhill. But that's what you get for using a guidebook notoriously prone to bouts of self-doubt and subjectivity.

The DEWSBURY ARM doesn't take prisoners. Your senses are sent down for assault and battery. Once, prior to construction of the Thornhill Cut, it formed a through route, rejoining the river to the north of its latter-day terminus at Savile Town. It is an unimaginative canal explorer, though, who can resist an arm's temptation. Go on, kill the cat with curiosity, push your prow past the cement works, the steel-holding yards, the scrap yards and the breezeblock yards to where the mosques and minarets of downtown Dewsbury look devoutly down upon its boat-filled terminus. Who knows, with luck, you may never come this way again.

Between Dewsbury and Mirfield the navigation continues to alternate between man-made cuts and river sections, making for fascinating contrasts, especially when boating. Gloomy as the THORNHILL CUT can be, it has its leavening moments: the handsome 1847 cast-iron span of

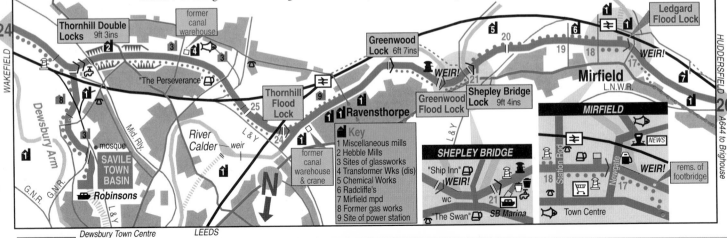

Key
1 Miscellaneous mills
2 Hebble Mills
3 Sites of glassworks
4 Transformer Wks (dis)
5 Chemical Works
6 Radcliffe's
7 Mirfield mpd
8 Former gas works
9 Site of power station

the London & North Western Railway; the Yorkshire Transformer Works, debauched by the decay of its redundantly pretentious concrete architecture; a stolid, stone-built warehouse; and the discarded Hebble Mills, overhanging the cutting above the Double Locks on a sequence of high rounded arches like something out of a surrealist painting by Chirico.

No other guidebook quite prepares you for the degeneracy of the Calder in the neighbourhood of Ravensthorpe. One of the mills around here became famous for supplying blankets to the red indians of North America. Now they probably provide dental floss to the man in the moon. Detritus spills out from riverside factories. A skeletal grey girder bridge spans the water. Morale becomes difficult to sustain.

GREENWOOD CUT breaches the trade descriptions act, being bordered by an industrial estate and sundry wastegrounds. A short curving section of river, with a broad weir, separates it from SHEPLEY BRIDGE. Note how the upstream section of each cut is protected by flood gates, whilst their lower ends feature conventional locks.

At Shepley Bridge an old boatbuilding yard, latterly used by British Waterways, enjoys a new lease of life as a hire base and provider of boating facilities. The MIRFIELD CUT is approximately a mile long. Some characterful properties and premises overlook the canal: saturnine Victorian villas, gaunt mills and (our favourite) the works of Squire A. Radcliffe & Sons, blenders of textile waste oils who occupy maltings separated from the towpath by a still-cobbled road. Mirfield Boat Yard also caught our eye, but as we went to press it closed down. Once it was the birthplace of wooden West Country keels; the last, "Isobel", being launched in 1955. Sister barge, the "Ethel" was preserved at the Boat Museum, Ellesmere Port. The drydock was originally the route of the navigation prior to opening of the Mirfield Cut.

Two sections of towpath are, to all intents and purposes, non existent, necessitating detours on to adjoining roads between Ravensthorpe and Shepley Bridge and Mirfield and Battye Ford (Map 26).

Ledgard Flood Lock

RUBBING off on you yet, the Calder & Hebble's elusive charm? Certainly the frequent juxtaposition of river navigation with canal cut keeps the adrenalin - as well as the Calder itself - flowing: in its 22 miles it falls over 190 feet through 27 locks. BATTYEFORD LOCK is overlooked by the "Pear Tree Inn" which has a mooring jetty for boating patrons just upstream from the entrance of the cut. Above the lock, the friendly South Pennine Boat Club occupy the site of a former boatbuilding yard whose drydock survives. On the neighbouring hillside, Mirfield Monastery, occupied by the Order of the Resurrection, stands aloof from the Calder Valley with its pale green rooftops. The church was built between 1910 and 1939 on the site of a former quarry, partially adapted as an open-air theatre. The adjoining house belonged to a family whose fortune was made selling blankets during the Franco-Prussian War. Bedding is still manufactured locally at the Nunbrook Mills overlooking the adjacent weir.

At COOPER BRIDGE the waters of one of the Calder's most significant tributaries, the Colne, make their presence felt amidst a plethora of sewage works. Robin Hood and Little John forded across the Calder hereabouts at the end of their ill-fated journey to Kirklees Priory in 1247, where the hero of Sherwood Forest is said to have been bled to death by the treacherous abbess.

The Colne and the Calder are not the only junction-makers at Cooper Bridge, for the Huddersfield Broad meets the Calder & Hebble here as well - see Map 26A. Islanded between the two navigable waterways stands an interesting, albeit mothballed, collection of wharf buildings overlooked by the high-chimnied mill of the Holme Spinning Company. 'Down South', on a more popular canal, it would make a wonderful base for a craft centre and tea rooms. Collectors of the obscure and enigmatic should stroll down the A643 to its junction with the A62 where the Dumb Steeple is a roadside monument to the efforts of local Luddites to jam the brakes on Progress. By

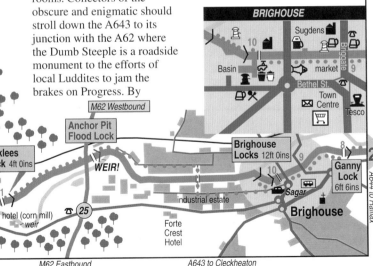

BATTYEFORD

15

South Pennine Boat Club

"Pear Tree"

A644

Cooper Bridge Lock No.1 (HB)

26A

A643 from Huddersfield

WEIR!

Cooper Bridge Flood Lock

Holme Spinning Co.

Battyeford Flood Lock

sewage works

sewage works

Cooper Bridge Lock (C&H) 5ft 3ins

14

13

25

15

weir

Battyeford Lock 8ft 3ins

Monastery   Bracken Hill

Little Chef

Robin Hood's Grave

N

Kirklees Lock 4ft 0ins

Kirklees Low Lock 9ft 3ins

11

hotel (corn mill)   *weir*

25

BRIGHOUSE

Sugdens

10

Basin

market

9

Bethel St.

Town Centre

Tesco

M62 Westbound

Anchor Pit Flood Lock

WEIR!

industrial estate

Brighouse Locks 12ft 0ins

9

10

Ganny Lock 6ft 6ins

8

2

Sagar

Brighouse

A644 to Halifax

Forte Crest Hotel

A62 to Leeds

M62 Eastbound

A643 to Cleckheaton

definition, a high proportion of canal travellers will be inclined to wish they had succeeded.

Hidden by woodland, Robin Hood's grave overlooks the KIRKLEES CUT, a refreshingly green interval between the urban impregnations of Cooper Bridge and Brighouse. Kirklees corn mill has been converted into an attractive hotel, but the unbridged river renders it inaccessible from the canal. Minor details kindle images of the past: a stone distance post marking 100 yards to the Low Lock; a curious horizontal wheel at the tail of Kirklees Lock which presumably had some function to do with the tow-rope of horse-drawn keels; and a Lancashire & Yorkshire Railway boundary stone recalling that the Calder & Hebble was once leased to this railway.

The M62 crosses the cut near its reunion with the river at Anchor Pit. Bumper to bumper, the volume of traffic apparent on its high-stilted crossing of the valley emphasises that the demand for Trans-Pennine trade continues, though it is a long time since this inland waterway was an integral part of the most expeditious method of transferring goods from Lancashire to Yorkshire.

Between Anchor Pit and Brighouse the highest navigable reach of the Calder creeps, somewhat uninspiringly, through a corridor of industrial premises; lucrative, no doubt, but mundane, like the "specialist in the reclamation of indexable toolings." Heaven help anyone who gets stuck next to one of their employees at a dinner party. By a bend in the river, two short terraces of stone housing apparently still depend on outside privvies.

BRIGHOUSE is a comely little town with a fetching waterfront. Eschewing the designated visitor moorings in the curving pool between the locks, we moored by Sugden's Mill and were lulled to sleep by the hum of mysterious machinery. But Brighouse Basin is equally splendid, and sundry satanic mills and warehouses provide a suitably demonic stage set for the unfolding of its cloth-capped charms.

Kirklees Cut

WE were not expecting much of the Huddersfield Broad, consequently we enjoyed it enormously. Firstly, though, we had to hit on its shy, low-profile egress from the Calder & Hebble in the neighbourhood of Cooper Bridge. Bottomley's mill chimney (aka Holme Spinning Co) serves as a useful landmark, but extreme caution is required from boaters if they are to avoid being drawn towards a sizeable weir on the Calder, immediately upstream of which, on the right hand side, lies the entrance lock to the Huddersfield Broad, beneath a slender towpath bridge bearing a triangular bridge plate numbered 'H5'.

LOCK No.1 is prettily overlooked by the keeper's cottage, invariably guarded by a large, but seemingly docile (well, from a distance, anyway) Dobermann. An interpretation board offers a few salient facts regarding the "Broad's" history and commercial use. Also known as Sir John Ramsden's Canal (after a local landowner instrument in its promotion) the canal sets off from Cooper Bridge on a surprisingly rural four mile journey into the heart of Huddersfield.

Passing under the main Trans-Pennine railway line, and negotiating Lock No.2, the canal slips through a water treatment works. A weird sculpture park of concrete pilings stands enigmatically alongside the towpath. On the misty morning of our first encounter with them, they resembled an Inca burial ground. The pound between locks 3 and 4 is framed by abandoned railway viaducts and overlooked by a large dyeworks which used to get its sulphur from Widnes by barge via the Rochdale Canal. The first viaduct, of fifteen blue brick arches, is a relic of the Midland Railway's ill-timed expansionism prior to the First World War. It belonged to the same misplaced optimism as the abandoned line between Calder Grove and Dewsbury which was to have speeded Anglo-Scottish traffic through the West Riding. The second viaduct, embellished with yellow brick eyebrows above its blue arches, carried the London & North Western Railway's "Kirkburton Dick" push & pull locals across the Colne Valley until they steamed into oblivion back in 1930. When the viaduct was being built, one of its arches fell into the canal on (make a note of this - we'll be asking questions later) the 1st February 1866.

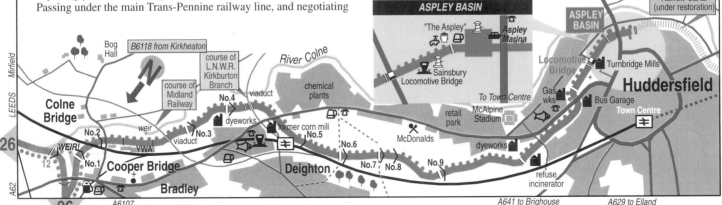

A former corn mill stands alongside the A62 road bridge at DEIGHTON. A most attractive pound ensues, with a swarthily wooded railway embankment on one side and an array of sports fields on the other. A notice board advises passers-by to keep an eye out for stray javelins. Locks materialise at frequent intervals as the canal traverses a quasi rural landscape interspersed with pockets of woodland and a continuing abundance of work's playing fields. Across the A62 the football teams get paid for playing at Huddersfield Town's futuristic Alfred McAlpine stadium. Herbert Chapman, manager here in the Twenties when 'Town' won the league championship three times in a row, would have approved. The high chimney of the municipal incinerator soars above the canal in a manner reminiscent of a similar installation on the Wolverhampton 'Twenty-One'.

Less than a mile to go now, and the old industries, which once took so much advantage of canal transport, close in about the cut, creating shadowy canyons of cargo-carrying memories. Dog-legging under Leeds Road and passing a gasworks, Waterloo Mills and a waterside church, the Huddersfield Broad reaches its most famous installation, the Locomotive (or Turnbridge) Bridge, a Heath Robinsonish contraption, 'designed' - if that is not too functional a verb in this circumstance - to lift for the passage of boats. The accompanying photograph depicts this marvellous little wonder of the waterways far more graphically than words can. A sanitary station key is required to unlock the structure, but operation is by hand with a winch.

Thereafter the canal approaches ASPLEY BASIN somewhat anti-climatically. Much of the old ambience has been swept away with the erection of a huge Sainsbury supermarket on one side and a modern pub on the other. At least their presence, and that of a small boatyard, provides a sense of security for mooring up to explore the entertaining town of Huddersfield. Historically, the Broad Canal continued for a quarter of a mile, making a connection with the River Colne. The Huddersfield Narrow Canal is another story altogether. Actively being restored, it is 'racing' across the hills to beat the Rochdale Canal to the honour of being the first to compliment the Leeds & Liverpool as a Trans-Pennine waterway.

Locomotive Bridge

ELLAND

King'tine gate

Ling'tine gate

Elland Bridge

60'

5

wc

"Barge & Barrel"

SALTERHEBBLE

Hebble Brook

WC

keeper

Halifax Branch

Main Line

P

PRE-INDUSTRIALLY, the Calder Valley must have been beguilingly beautiful. Here and there echoes of this long forgotten rustic charm remain intact: a luxuriantly wooded hillside to the north; a sprinkling of farms between the factories. And so all kinds of oddly juxtaposed images catch the eye: beef cattle fattening against a factory wall; a pair of disused lock-keepers offices; sundry distance posts made of stone; a ruined lock connecting with the river; the as yet undemolished cooling towers of Elland's abandoned power station; some flooded gravel pits; but most provocatively, a two chimnied salute from the tree-tops

Elland Town Centre

Woodside Mills Lock 6ft 9ins

4

Dobson's Sweet Factory

Ely Garnett

A629 from Huddersfield

maltings (dis)

mills

5

mills

Longlees Lock 6ft 6ins

Elland Lock 6ft 9ins

NEWS

crematorium

Park Nook Lock 7ft 0ins

"Collier's Arms"

power station (dis)

weir

60'

"Rawson Arms"

Knowles Pipeworks

site of old lock

Cromwell Lock 6ft 0ins

6

Cromwell Bottom

Calderdale Way

Brookfoot Lock 5ft 0ins

site of old lock

26

weir

Brookfoot

Salterhebble Locks 25ft 0ins

Exley

"Punch Bowl"

"The Quays" (Premier Lodge)

A629 to Halifax (2 miles)

Course of Halifax Branch & "Hebble Trail"

sewage works

60'

weir (model industrial settlement)

Copley

foundry

viaduct

weir

Sterne Bridge

3

2

Halifax Bud. Soc.

by the Ash Grove Works of W.T. Knowles, seemingly the last manufacturers in Britain of good old fashioned, salt glazed sanitary pipes. ELLAND injects further urban character straight into the canal traveller's veins. Tall mills rear up behind the refurbished wharf like security men attempting, unconvincingly, to protect a VIP yet remain in the shadows. A small personal aside: the railway is currently (temporarily, one hopes) without passenger services, but back in 1967 your author went AWOL from his school speech day, in order to ride on one of the last steam-hauled, Summer Saturday Bridlington-Bradford holiday trains, which puffed across the canal at this point, moments before taking on a banker at Greetland for the stiff and cacophonous climb up to Halifax.
The trio of locks at SALTERHEBBLE are arguably the most picturesque on the Calder & Hebble. They are laid out around a dog-leg curve. The top two were once a staircase, whilst the bottom lock features an unusual,

electrically-operated (out with your sanitary station key) guillotine gate at its tail, an introduction necessitated by widening of the adjacent road bridge. We were interested to see that the gate was manufactured by Ransome & Rapier of Ipswich, a firm perhaps better known, in transport enthusiast circles at least, for their railway turntables. And, yes, we did manage to get it jammed, an embarrassing incident resulting in our wakening of the lock-keeper from his Saturday afternoon snooze. The secret, apparently, is to ensure that the conventional mitred gates at the top of the lock are tightly shut before attempting to operate the guillotine!

In the short pound between the middle and lower locks, a small aqueduct spans the Calder & Hebble's junior partner; a shy, retiring sort of chap called Hebble Brook, who springs to life on t'moors above Halifax. Time was when a branch canal climbed through fourteen locks in less than two miles to reach the centre of that sooty, hill-bounded textile and engineering town. Even as canals go, it was a heavy drinker. And because the local mills already had the valley's water supplies sewn up, water for the branch was pumped (at the rate of a thousand gallons a minute) up from the main line in an Escher-like arrangment of perpetual motion. Opened in 1828, the Halifax Branch became one of the less publicised abandonments of the LMS Railway's infamous 1944 Act, and much of its course has subsequently been obliterated, though you get some idea of its topography from the right hand side of a slow-climbing Sowerby Bridge-Halifax train, or more intimately by walking or cycling the "Hebble Trail", an enlivening, traffic-free right of way between the foreshortened terminus of the branch and the centre of Halifax. We were

amused to discover that one of the branch's more notable cargoes was 'goux', a euphemism for domestic sewage, exported to the East Riding and Lincolnshire for use as fertilizer. A few hundred yards of the Halifax Branch remains in water at the Salterhebble end, with a bustling modern pub called "The Quays" with visitor moorings providing reason enough for a short detour.

Between Salterhebble and Sterne Bridge the canal rides above a valley floor littered with sewage plants and factory premises. The Calder's flanks, however, are sylvan enough to create a favourable impression with those who like their inland waterway journeys on the pretty side. A many arched stone viaduct carries the Manchester-Bradford railway across the Calder & Hebble at Copley, a community based on a model mill village of 19th century worker's housing down by the riverside.

Its church stands on the opposite bank, masked by woodland, through which pleasant footpaths run. Canalside, acrid smoke billows from Kaye's Foundry. What on earth, the female members of our crew wanted insatiably to know, goes on in the 'fettling' department here?

The mill at Sterne Bridge, now used by a wire manufacturing company, belonged to the Sterne family of novelist Laurence fame, writer of that rambling18th century novel "Tristam Shandy". Another literary connection here relates to Wordsworth's poem "Lucy Gray", which was inspired by an incident involving the drowning of a young girl when the bridge was swept away by a winter flood. At the end of the poem, Wordsworth suggests that Lucy Gray is still to be seen: 'smoothly tripping along, singing a solitary song, and whistling in the wind'. Look out for her!

Salterhebble

REACHING Sowerby Bridge, the Calder & Hebble goes into a telephone box, puts its underpants on outside its trousers, and emerges as the Rochdale Canal, Superman of the inland waterways, fully equipped to take on the tyrannical Pennines. Sowerby basin provides an effective backdrop for this transformation scene. Here, in the early 19th century heyday of Trans-Pennine carriage by water, Mersey Flats exchanged their cargoes with West Country Keels because the Lancashire vessels were, at 70ft long, too large to negotiate the Calder & Hebble's stumpy locks. Such delays did little to help the canals compete with the emerging railways. Trade was abandoned across the summit of the Rochdale Canal before the Second World War, whilst the last waterborne cargo to reach Sowerby Bridge from the east was paper pulp on the keel "Frugality" in September 1955.

Not even a fortune-teller would have dared suggest that, forty years later, the Calder & Hebble and Rochdale canals would be relinked, but that was the almost miraculous turn of events, as this guidebook went to press, and we are working on the assumption that the obstacle at Tuel Lane (scheduled for removal by the end of 1995) has gone by the time you read this.

The Calder & Hebble approaches Sowerby Bridge from the east clinging to a shelf above the Calder. Cuddled in shallow hawthorn cuttings, or raised above the river on sappling-framed embankments, the inland waterway traveller's perspective is curtailed, creating a sense of intimacy that intensifies one's relationship with the canal. The hills and mills and railway lines provide reminders of the Upper Peak Forest Canal, but the most spectacular sight on this length is Wainhouse's Tower, an astonishing 253ft high tower of blackened ashlar stone, erected as a chimney for a dyeworks, though never used as such and later converted into a viewing tower. Open to the public on selected dates, 403 steps will take you to the top where, they always said, you could see Blackpool on a clear day, but days were seldom clear in the smoky West Riding of years gone by. In the Twenties it was employed, somewhat bizarrely, as a transmission tower for a local wireless station.

Sowerby Bridge basin retains a good deal of the latent atmosphere of trade. It was here that Dennis Waterman did his best to seduce Jan Francis aboard her residential keel in the

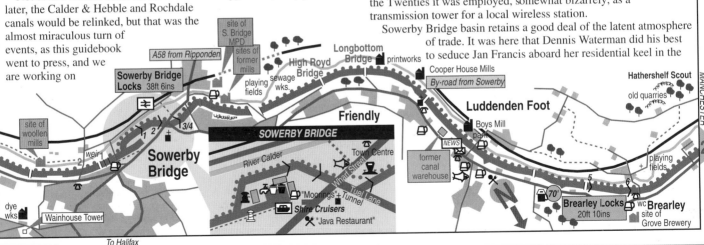

television series "Stay Lucky". But it is the architecture of the stone warehouses and the boat busy basin - where the Calder & Hebble terminated in 1770 pending the Rochdale's arrival from Lancashire in 1811 - which seduces the rest of us.

The Rochdale Canal swerves past the terminal basin and immediately declares its intention to conquer the Pennines by negotiating a pair of original locks (the first being named after Albert Wood, once the canal's principal trader) followed by one new, and very, very deep lock replacing two earlier chambers. The new lock was part of the Tuel Lane project reconnecting the Rochdale to the Calder & Hebble following development over the original course of the canal.

Running on a ledge between the river and its steep-sided valley, beneath the engagingly-named suburb of Friendly, the Rochdale enjoys an atypical paucity of locks, a pound extending to all of two and a half miles, which westbound boaters will grow to cherish with nostalgia and affection. A purer, decanted version of Calderdale seems to accompany the Rochdale as opposed to the Calder & Hebble. The mundane accoutrements of modern Britain are filtered out by the encroaching valley slopes, as if a darker, almost necromantic enchantment is hidden in these folds of millstone grit. Branwell Bronte, the literary sister's ne'er-do-well brother, was briefly station clerk at LUDDENDEN FOOT, and must have been familiar with, if hardly a habitue of, the gaunt, clock-towered United Reform Church overlooking the canal by Cooper House Mills, and with barges loading at the handsome, four-storey stone warehouse occupied by a camping gear stockist overlooking Boys Park. The past may well, as L.P. Hartley put it, be a

Sowerby Bridge

'foreign country', but there are cheap package tours departing daily if you have the imagination to join them.

BREARLEY LOCKS lie in an attractive setting overlooked by woods and adjacent to an ancient stone bridge spanning the Calder. The lower lock is called Edward Kilner after one of the company's engineers. Rochdale locks were 'standardised', as far as feasible, at between nine and ten feet rise so as to simplify the construction of gates and permit them to be interchangable. Follow the lane across the river, past another sizeable, if less ostentatious and now secularly used, chapel, and public footpaths will take you up on to the quarried face of Hathershelf Scout. Indeed, a good deal of the charm of a boating trip along the heavily-locked Rochdale Canal, lies with the opportunity, every now and then, for you to moor and rest your paddle-gear-weary muscles and walk up on to the neighbouring ridges. Up there the world - or at least this part of the mid-Pennines - is your oyster, and the views can be intoxicating.

Playing fields border the canal on the outskirts of MYTHOLMROYD as the Calder slips unnoticed behind an estate of industrial units. Its name means 'river of stones or hard water', and it makes a journey of over fifty miles from its source above Todmorden to its confluence with the Aire at Castleford. The local amateur dramatic society were presenting "Oklahoma" when we passed through. "We know we belong to the land, and the land we belong to is grand." Calderdale in a nutshell.

CALDERDALE narrows in a westerly direction like a duck decoy. Railway, road, canal and river are packed evermore tightly together as if they were a quartet of buxom farmwives on the back seat of a market day bus. MYTHOLMROYD has connections with the 18th century 'coiners' who operated a counterfeit mint in this inaccessible moorland location. They still make clogs at Walkley's canalside mill at Falling Royd, but the customers, these days, are tourists rather than millworkers. A horse-drawn trip boat operates between here and Hebden Bridge, creating an entertaining time-warp, a cosy Hovis-ad perception of the 19th century when boats were yanked along t'cut by 'animals' and folk were shod in clogs through economic necessity rather than nostalgia.

HEBDEN BRIDGE embraces the canal with an uncharacteristic show of emotion by West Riding standards. Prodigal sons returning to these parts are expected to supply their own fatted calves. But Calderdale folk seem genuinely pleased to have a navigable canal back in their midst and, overlooked by the main thoroughfare (the Halifax-Burnley trunk road) the revitalised basin (or marina, as they seem to prefer) has become the cynosure of every day-outer's eye. Waterbuses and tug trips are well established facets of local boating only too pleased to share their canal with inquistive explorers from the east.

The setting could hardly be bettered. With a backdrop of the town's leap-frogging buildings, the twin-armed and cobbled wharf is followed, to the west, by a lock, then a low, four arch aqueduct across the Calder adjacent to its confluence with the Hebden Water. Hebble End Works is occupied by various visitor attractions and craft outlets. Boaters are asked to leave the lower of the Stubbings Locks empty,

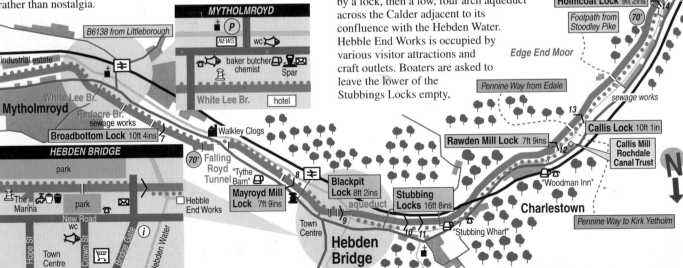

presumably its contents might otherwise leak into the cellars of the adjoining terrace houses.

Stephenson's Manchester & Leeds Railway crosses the Rochdale Canal at CHARLESTOWN. West of here the canal becomes more introverted: wizened trees waltz down to its southern bank; the Calder, coursing over its rocky bed is hard to equate with its navigable status below Brighouse. Scattered industrial premises emphasise the canal's role in kick-starting the valley's early 19th century economy. The steepness of the valley sides curtails most views of the moorlands on either flank. Weather-splattered wildernesses of peat bogs and moss are up there unseen, shadowing your progress along the valley's gutter-like floor. But abseiling down to cross the canal by Callis Lock, the Pennine Way rubber-stamps its seal of approval on your journey. Forty-two soggy miles south of here lies Edale, the Pennine Way's southern extremity.

Callis Mill is home base for the Rochdale Canal Trust who are in the slightly tortuous position of being responsible for the navigable upkeep of the canal whilst ownership remains with the original, never nationalised, canal company. They got so much practice making lock-gates for the revitalised Rochdale, that now they make them for other restoration projects such as the Grantham and Chesterfield canals.

Hebden Bridge

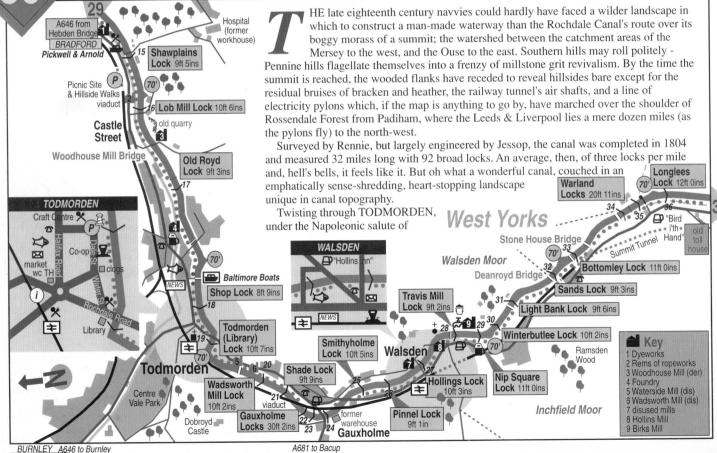

THE late eighteenth century navvies could hardly have faced a wilder landscape in which to construct a man-made waterway than the Rochdale Canal's route over its boggy morass of a summit; the watershed between the catchment areas of the Mersey to the west, and the Ouse to the east. Southern hills may roll politely - Pennine hills flagellate themselves into a frenzy of millstone grit revivalism. By the time the summit is reached, the wooded flanks have receded to reveal hillsides bare except for the residual bruises of bracken and heather, the railway tunnel's air shafts, and a line of electricity pylons which, if the map is anything to go by, have marched over the shoulder of Rossendale Forest from Padiham, where the Leeds & Liverpool lies a mere dozen miles (as the pylons fly) to the north-west.

Surveyed by Rennie, but largely engineered by Jessop, the canal was completed in 1804 and measured 32 miles long with 92 broad locks. An average, then, of three locks per mile and, hell's bells, it feels like it. But oh what a wonderful canal, couched in an emphatically sense-shredding, heart-stopping landscape unique in canal topography.

Twisting through TODMORDEN, under the Napoleonic salute of

West Yorks

Map labels:

29 — A646 from Hebden Bridge
BRADFORD
Pickwell & Arnold
Hospital (former workhouse)
15 Shawplains Lock 9ft 5ins
70'
Picnic Site & Hillside Walks viaduct
P
2
16 Lob Mill Lock 10ft 6ins
old quarry
3
Castle Street
Woodhouse Mill Bridge
17 Old Royd Lock 9ft 3ins
TODMORDEN
Craft Centre
Co-op
market wc TH
clogs
Halifax Road
Dale St
Water St
Rochdale Road
Library
4
70'
Baltimore Boats
Shop Lock 8ft 9ins
18
19 Todmorden (Library) Lock 10ft 7ins
70'
Todmorden
5
6 20
Shade Lock 9ft 9ins
Wadsworth Mill Lock 10ft 2ins
21 viaduct
Gauxholme Locks 30ft 2ins
22 23 24
Gauxholme
Dobroyd Castle
Centre Vale Park
BURNLEY A646 to Burnley
A681 to Bacup

WALSDEN
"Hollins Inn"
NEWS
Travis Mill Lock 9ft 2ins
Smithyholme Lock 10ft 5ins
Walsden
Walsden Moor
31
28
+ 9 29 30
8 7
27 Hollings Lock 10ft 3ins
25
26
Pinnel Lock 9ft 1in
former warehouse
Nip Square Lock 11ft 0ins
Ramsden Wood
Inchfield Moor

Stone House Bridge
Deanroyd Bridge
Warland Locks 20ft 11ins
Longlees Lock 12ft 0ins
70'
34
35 36
"Bird i'th Hand"
old toll house
3
70' 33
Summit Tunnel
32
Bottomley Lock 11ft 0ins
Sands Lock 9ft 3ins
Light Bank Lock 9ft 6ins
Winterbutlee Lock 10ft 2ins
70'

Key
1 Dyeworks
2 Rems of ropeworks
3 Woodhouse Mill (der)
4 Foundry
5 Waterside Mill (dis)
6 Wadsworth Mill (dis)
7 disused mills
8 Hollins Mill
9 Birks Mill

Stoodley Pike, which sits like a rocket about to be launched on the moors, the canal bids hail and farewell to the Calder, and passes beneath the 'Great Wall of Todmorden' (a massive blue brick retaining wall supporting the adjoining railway) before climbing assiduously through sundry settlements of herring-bone-terraced housing and fish-scale-coloured weaving sheds. This is the fag end of the twentieth century for goodness sake, but in Gauxholme and Walsden (where a little mill shop will still sell you a pair of 'breeks' as opposed to trousers) it might still be the eighteenth. Cobbled alleys support washing lines. Heathery banks, in the process of being rapidly colonised by rhododendrons, climb to ridges delineated by drystone walling. As the valley's shoulders converge, there is barely elbow room for the lines of communication to forge their way towards the summit. The most potent image of this conflict is at GAUXHOLME, where the railway works a 'one-two' with the canal, one of its crossings being a Gothically inspired, cast iron bridge with crenellated abutments as photogenic from the neighbouring hillside, as anything anywhere on the inland waterway system. By the top of the Gauxholme Three a handsome warehouse with arched loading bay stands alongside the canal.

Locks with lovely names like Nip Square and Winterbutlee lift the Rochdale out of a landscape of mills into a landscape of sheep and isolated hill farms. The short intervening pounds have a predilection for loosening their stays and spilling over into fleshy, reedy margins. Presumably this was an aid to water supply, along with the canal company's eight reservoirs which gleam like aluminium up on the moorland tops. Given the notorious inclination to rain that this part of the world 'enjoys', it is hard to conceive that water supply was ever a problem. But, it was, and in their heyday the reservoirs supplied up to four million gallons a day to the canal through a network of feeder channels. All the reservoirs were sold to the Rochdale and Oldham corporations in 1923, on the understanding that sufficient water levels would be maintained on the canal. Not that such supplies were needed much longer in the cause of navigation, for the last through barge crossed the summit in the Thirties. Now the reservoirs are the 'property' of a privatised utility, and negotiations are proceeding for the Canal Trust to purchase sufficient supplies for the anticipated increase in boat usage that reconnection to the rest of the canal system will bring.

The summit is as brief as this sentence. If, at 601 feet above sea level, there is a higher stretch of navigable canal in the country, we can't think of it. The adjoining railway, engineered by George Stephenson only forty years after completion of the canal, tunnels under the highest point of the gorge in order to reduce the steepness of its approach gradients. Diesels hoot hauntingly as they enter the tunnel's decorated portals, contributing to the sense of isolation. The old Todmorden Turnpike road passes a toll house at Warland where West Yorkshire gives way, as gracefully as possible in the circumstances, to Greater Manchester.

Gauxholme

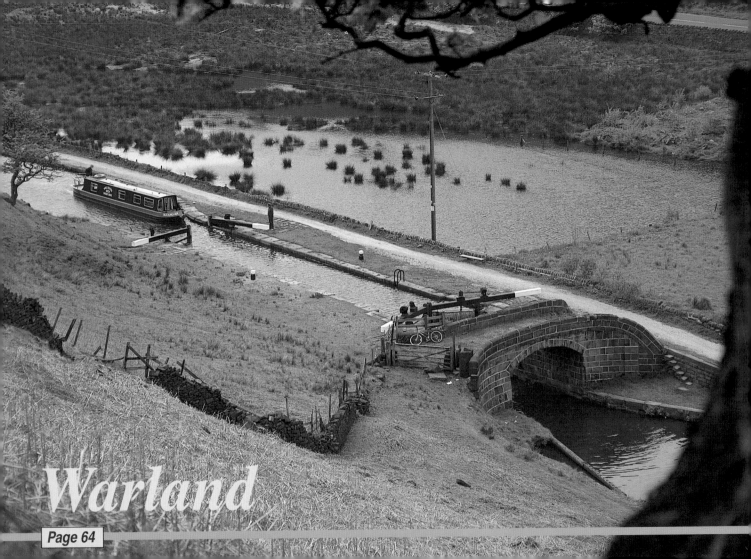

Warland

JUST as a stranger can find it difficult to differentiate between the accents and dialects of Lancashire and Yorkshire, so too is it hard to draw a distinction between the landscapes. Closer scrutiny suggested a tendency to austerity at the western end of the summit level, a greater inclination to use brick which lacks the warmth and harmony of local stone. But perhaps it was simply the rain, descending like nine inch galvanised nails, which coloured our perceptions as we came down from the six hundred feet contour on our initial research trip, senses still reeling from the high octane entertainment provided by this spectacular canal.

With the little River Roch in tow, the Rochdale Canal gets quickly 'stuck in', as a series of locks carry it down past the old Rock Nook cotton mills now occupied by Courtaulds Aerospace. Did you notice how the Roch is taken over the railway by the western portal of Summit Tunnel on an iron trough?

We keep referring to this as 'Lancashire', but since the crass local government reorganisations of the mid Seventies, no part of the Rochdale Canal lies in Lancashire at all! Here, heaven help us, we're in Greater Manchesterland. The canal does its best to rise above the imperfections of political boundaries, although it is noticeable that the locks are less well-appointed on this side, lacking nameplates and benches for the resting of weary, balance-beam-bruised bottoms. The cast iron mileposts also appear to have petered out, but perhaps we have simply gotten ahead of a rolling programme of improvements blowing in from the east.

By Benthouse Lock a slender, angled dock complete with stump of crane hints at former commerce. Although shown on the 1911, 6in OS map, no corresponding works caught our eye. Perhaps there was some intercourse with Stephenson's new fangled railway, or with the quarry at nearby Windy Bank. Several mills have disappeared. Durn Mill dealt, unusually for Lancashire, in woollens.

The outskirts of Littleborough turn a somewhat blank face towards the Rochdale Canal's abrupt loss of navigable status, like a potential witness anxious not to get involved in describing the events leading up to an accident. There are no signs to tell you that this is the 'end of the line'. Though you don't need to hail from Harley Street to confirm that this particular patient's heart has stopped beating. The B6225 from Milnrow skews across the cut at water level, overlooked with undisguised irony by a little pub called "The Railway".

One day this canal (and our guide) will take you on down the remaining 17 miles and 35 locks to Manchester. Meanwhile, after a quick Bass, we're winding t'boat and heading back to Wigan - the long way.

Chelburn Moor

A58 from Halifax

Pikehouse Lock 10ft 3ins

Sladen Lock 10ft 3ins

Sladen Bridge

Thickone Lock 10ft 2ins

Benthouse Bridge

Durn Lock 9ft 9ins

Summit Locks 30ft 9ins

Summit Level 600ft

Littleborough Bottom Lock 10ft 1ins

Punchbowl Locks 31ft 0ins

R. Roch

Benthouse Lock 9ft 7ins

LITTLEBOROUGH

"The Summit"

Summit

Littleborough

Calderbrook

chemical wks

"The Railway"

B6225 from Milnrow

Greater Manchester

Lo-Cost

NEWS

wc

To Rochdale 2miles

Coach House

"Falcon Inn"

A58 to Rochdale (2mls)

laundrette

ADLINGTON

Map 2

Adlington's usefulness to boaters is multipled by the provision of designated visitor moorings alongside the recreation ground south of bridge 69. The village is also the most practical canalside base camp for the ascent of Rivington Pike a couple of country miles to the east.

MARINERS COFFEE SHOP is housed in the old station booking hall: coffees, light lunches and teas, plus a take-away service. Similarly, the BUTTY SHOP on the main street serves take-away hot pies and sandwiches all day long to a wide cross-secton of passing workers. The best appointed pub is the WHITE BEAR - again on the main road - which usefully offers accommodation (01257-482357).

SPAR store at crossroads 200 yards from bridge 69. Also nearby are a chemist, newsagent and post office.

TRAINS: from station half mile east of bridge 69, hourly, daily to/from Manchester, Preston and Blackpool. Tel: 01772-259439.
BUSES: local services along A6 corridor. Tel: 01257-241693.

RIVINGTON COUNTRY PARK: 2 miles east of Adlington. Reservoirs, signposted walks, gardens and breathtaking views.

BARNOLDSWICK

Map 10

'Barlick", as the locals call it, looks less than inviting from the canal, but its centre, 10 minutes walk from bridges 153 or 154A, is very pleasant indeed, being gathered about the Town Square, a modern renovation on the site of the old Co-op.

ANCHOR INN (Salterforth - bridge 151): cheerful stone pub pre-dating canal with stalactites in the cellar. Bass & bar meals; families welcome. Numerous other pubs and cafes in 'Barlick' with fish & chips adjacent bridge 153.

Corner shop near bridge 153, otherwise head for the centre where there's a LEO'S (Co-op) supermarket and a mouthwatering array of baker and butcher shops. Branches of Midland, TSB, Barclay & Yorkshire banks.

BUSES: Pennine services link with Skipton & Colne. Tel: 01756-749215.

TOURIST INFORMATION: Fernlea Ave. Tel: 01282-817046.
BANCROFT MILL: preserved compound stationary steam engine. Regular steaming afternoons. Tel: 01282-813932.

BARROWFORD

Map 9

Attractively strung-out along the banks of Pendle Water, Barrowford lies a worthwhile quarter of an hour's walk along a pavemented road to the west of bridge 143A

GEORGE & DRAGON: opp Heritage Centre. John Smith's, food etc.
PARK CHIPPY excellent. See also Heritage Centre Garden Tea Room below for coffees, light lunches and teas.

Local shops cater for most requirements. Bannisters Bakery is especially good.

BUSES: frequent services to/from Nelson. Tel: 01282-698533.

PENDLE HERITAGE CENTRE: Park Hill. Tel: 01282-695366. Open daily 10am-4.30pm. Fascinating and atmospheric interpretive centre for Pendle past and present. Shop, tea rooms, garden and woodland walk.

BINGLEY

Map 16

The A650's seamless traffic does Bingley few favours, and it remains to be seen whether the new Airedale road will provide any balm. But away from the busy main street, Bingley has its quiet places: a pleasant riverside park, an interesting and substantial parish church, and an old Butter Cross thought to date from 1212 when King John first granted a market charter.

THE FISHERMANS - canalside bridge 205. Popular with boaters, walkers and, yes, fishermen, alike. Bass beers and bar meals (except for Sunday) BROWN COW - congenial riverside pub with nice, dark wood-panelled interior by Ireland Bridge. Bar & restaurant meals. Timothy Taylor ales. Accommodation. Tel: 01274 -569482.

Market on Weds & Fris. Branches of most banks. SAFEWAY supermarket adjacent to canal. DAMART factory shop on Park Road.

TRAINS: frequent Metro local services linking Bingley with Skipton, Saltaire, Shipley, Bradford & Leeds. V. useful for towpath walkers.

BLACKBURN Map 5

The chief of East Lancashire's old textile towns doesn't exactly inspire confidence as a place to drop anchor, but there's more to Blackburn than meets the average, motorised, tourist's eye, and by the time you've retraced your steps to the canal, you may find your preconceptions falling away.

CARROTTS - Temple Court (adjacent to Cathedral). Charming bistro housed in former ironmongery and named after the owner's cat. Emphasis on wholesome vegetarian food served at tables squeezed between craft displays. Saturday evening menu but closed Sundays. Tel: 01254-582738. In our opinion one of the best half dozen eating places listed in this guide.

Shopping is one of Blackburn's strongpoints, from the fine MARKET HALL to TOMMY BALL'S shoe superstore. There are Asda, Morrisons and Tesco supermarkets all within supermarket trolley submerging distance of the canal.

TRAINS - frequent connections with major centres throughout the region. Handy services along the L&L Corridor via Rishton, Church, Hapton, Rose Grove, Burnley, Brierfield and Nelson to Colne. Tel: 01772-259439.
BUSES - direct link with Chorley, otherwise not available by train. Ribble service 123/4, hourly, daily. Tel: 01772-254754.

(i) TOURIST INFORMATION - Northgate. Tel: 01254-53277. Major visitor attractions include WAVES, an indoor pool with wave simulation and flume; the ARENA ice rink; the ART GALLERY and LEWIS TEXTILE MUSEUM; and the late nineteenth century CATHEDRAL.

BRIGHOUSE Map 26

Best known for its brass band, Brighouse is an engaging little town with a network of largely traffic-free streets made up of shot-blasted clean Victorian stone buildings. Not a lot of people know that Wagner's grand-daughters went to school here.

Down to earth pubs on most street corners. Several fish & chip shops within "bring 'em back hot, mind" reach of the canal. LA ROMANTICA Italian restaurant adjacent to canal basin on Mill Lane. SWANKIES is an attractive cafe on Bethel St offering such gastronomic delights as Belgian (but why not "Brighouse"?) Flan.

Shopping is an enjoyable pastime here and many independent retailers, like BRAYSHAWS ("the pork pie specialist") on Bethel Street and CZERWIK'S wine & cheese shop on Commercial St seem to thrive. Brighouse is big enough to support branches of Woolworths, Boots and Tesco and there are NatWest, Barclays and Midland banks.

BUSES - to most West Riding destinations. Tel: 01422-364467. No railway station at present.

BURNLEY Map 8

Under a canopy of stars, with the streetlights twinkling across the canal, and a frosty wind searing off the Pennines, Burnley's backdrop of mills and chimneys looked much as it might have done three-quarters of a century ago. Daylight, though, exposed the town's post industrial shortcomings: tailbacks on the inner ring-road, litter wafting through the precinct; a hollow, underfed emptiness behind the textile mill windows. But we liked Burnley: its imposing municipal buildings, the Ashfield Road viaduct (railway equivalent of the canal embankment spanning the valley of the Brun) and the population's determinaton to 'get on with life' despite being just a mile or two too far down the M65 to ever fully experience the miracle of industrial regeneration.

BELFIELD'S - prize winning fish & chips by Finsley Gate Wharf. THE MECHANICS - Manchester Road. Arts Centre bar serving the town's excellent Moorhouse ales.

Modern precinct and traffic-free street shopping as befits the "fourth largest centre in Lancashire". Fine MARKET HALL (Mon-Sat) plus open air stalls on Mon, Thur & Sat. SAINSBURY supermarket adjacent to canal embankment, ASDA by Central rly sta.

TRAINS: services from Central & Barracks stations to/from Colne & Blackburn. Services from Manchester Road to/from Yorkshire. Tel: 01772-259439. BUSES - Tel: 01282-425244.

(i) TOURIST INFORMATION - Manchester Road. Tel: 01282 455485. WEAVERS TRIANGLE VISITOR CENTRE - Manchester Road (bridge 130B). Open Easter-Sep, Mon-Wed, Sat & Sun afternoons. Tel: 01282-452403.

CALDER GROVE
Map 24

THE NAVIGATION - canalside below Broad Cut Top Lock. Splendid stone-built inn separated from water's edge by large garden with picnic tables and childrens play area. Inside, it's divided into two distinct zones: a quiet and cosy lounge hung with archive photographs of the Calder & Hebble; and a family bar complete with 'ball play' area. The beer includes Timothy Taylor's nectar from Keighley, whilst amongst a wide menu of bar meals lurks the locally made Hector Ellis pork pie, best taken with mushy peas. Another of our top six!

Small general store, newsagents and post office on main road five minutes walk uphill.

CASTLEFORD
Map 21

A tough little town with a tough outlook befitting its status a centre for heroic deeds in the world of Rugby League. The town centre lies a bleak, but interesting quarter of an hour's walk across the Aire from the Visitor Moorings in Bulholme Cut, though there are modest shopping facilities on Lock Lane. Henry Moore, the sculptor, was born in Castleford, but its prosperity has been derived from making glass and chemicals. On your way into town, look out for Allinson's flour mill. In common with their famous stoneground bread, Castleford is a "town with n'out taken out!"

THE GRIFFIN - Lock Lane. One of our haunts from barge-watching days. Photos of Rugby League heros on the walls and a nice line in inexpensive bar food. John Smith's beers.

Surprisingly substantial shopping centre called Carlton Lanes in the heart of town, but it's a long way back over Castleford Bridge with packages unless you can be bothered to unravel the local bus timetable.

TRAINS - local services to/from Leeds & Wakefield.
BUSES - ditto!

CHORLEY
Map 3

Cakes are Chorley's claim to fame, a sticky, fruity pastry of the Eccles ilk much favoured locally, but difficult to find elsewhere. And sadly, the centre of town is perhaps just too far from the canal for the average boater to take much notice of it, though there are points of interest, such as Tuesday's "Flat Iron" market and Astley Hall, a 16th century mansion owned by the local authority, which demand further investigation.

RAILWAY HOTEL - canalside bridge 78A. "Brewers Fayre" pub open 'all day' for food. Families welcome.

COLNE
Map 9

Hilltop town, two miles east of Barrowford Locks, notable for its "British in India" museum (01282-870215) devoted to the great days of the Raj. Colne was the home of Wallace Hartley, conductor of the "Titanic's" heroic band who played "Nearer My God to Thee" as the liner went down. But Colne's main use to users of this guide is likely to be perceived as that of a staging-post with useful transport facilities for towpath walkers.

TRAINS - terminus of branch from Burnley Central, daily service running through to Blackpool. Tel: 01772-259439.
BUSES - connections with Skipton via Barnoldswick. Tel: 01756-749215.

DEWSBURY
Map 25

Typical West Riding wollen town, best known these days for the large retail market (where the emphasis is still very much on textiles) held on Wednesdays and Saturdays The town centre lies across the Calder, about twenty minutes trudge from Savile Town Basin.

EAST MARTON
Map 11

Heavenly stopover high up in the Dales with, appropriately enough, a lovely church with a Norman tower, though the interior was much 'improved' by the Victorians. Moor the boat and stretch your legs along the "Pennine Way".

CROSS KEYS - overlooking bridge 161 (though quieter approach from 162). Classic country pub offering a wonderfully varied menu of bar and restaurant food. Black Sheep on draught. Families catered for.
ABBOT'S HARBOUR - adjacent bridge 162. Delightful cafe/restaurant also dealing in postcards, local books, confectionary etc.

ELLAND
Map 27

Characterful little industrial town on a hill above the Calder. The bridge dates back to the 17th century, though with subsequent lengthenings and widenings. Notable businesses include Dobson's sweet factory and Ely Garnett & Son, "providers of wool noils, laps and waste". Look out for the Rex Cinema, a survivor from the pre-multiscreen age.

COLLIERS ARMS - canalside below Elland Lock. The landlord is a boatowner himself and couldn't have been more helpful to our research crew marooned without running water. Sam Smith's beer and bar meals served in an attractive conservatory overlooking the canal. Childrens room and moorings for patrons. Other pubs popular with canal users include the BARGE & BARREL at Elland Wharf and the RAWSON ARMS reached (though not by towpath walkers) through the woods from Rawson's Pool below Park Nook Lock.

Elland provides good shopping facilities and gravity should aid your package-laden progress back to the boat. Branches of Lloyds, Yorkshire, NatWest and Barclays banks. Co-op supermarket, bookshop, delicatessen etc. Dobson's retail sweety shop on Southgate.

FOULRIDGE
Map 9

A deservedly popular overnight stop for boaters, Foulridge marks the westernmost limit of many a hire boat itinerary before industry begins to make an impression. The village itself is indeed a attractive base from which to explore the surrounding countryside, and there are many pleasant walks to be had in the vicinity of the canal's reservoirs. Our research crew were intrigued to see the lady from the tea rooms taking her two ferrets for a walk on a lead. A trip boat operates public services on Sundays and Tuesdays throughout the season. Tel: 01282-870241.

The HOLE IN THE WALL celebrates the adventures of 'Buttercup' the amphibious cow, but 'our lot' went up to the main road, bearing right until they fell off the edge of the map, to the HARE & HOUNDS, and treated themselves (no expense spared) to fillet steaks washed down with Tetley's bitter. Back canalside, the TEA ROOMS provide "traditional and Victorian cuisine" daily (January excepted) and are also open on Thursday & Saturday evenings. (Tel: 01282-869159. There is also a fish & chip shop.

Newsagents & general store, off licence and butcher. CROFT MILL SHOP sells a variety of fabrics. Tel: 01282-869625.

Pennine Motors link Foulridge with Barnoldswick, Colne and Skipton. Tel: 01756-749215.

GARGRAVE
Map 12

If Skipton is the Leeds & Liverpool Canal's nicest town, Gargrave qualifies as its most pleasant large village. It has set out its stall to cater for visitors ever since the inception of the Pennine Way, and now welcomes discerning canal users, whether they be on foot or afloat, as well. Leaving one of the crew to replenish the water tank, we went in search of ice cream and came upon a village which quickly captivated us with its charming houses. Deeper into the heart of things we found the Aire lapping at the edge of an elongated green and discovered the premises of Pennine Motors, the bus operator with the distinctive fleet of orange and grey coloured coaches.

ANCHOR INN - canalside bridge 169A. Busy 'Brewers Fayre' family pub with extensive gardens. Accommodation. Tel: 01756-749666.
WOODS BISTRO - village centre. Quaint and relatively inexpensive eating house open evenings and Sun lunch. Tel: 01756-749252.
DALESMAN CAFE - village centre - high starch meals for hungry cyclists and walkers.
EDMONDSONS - good old-fashioned chip shop (not Mons).

Useful range of shops including small supermarket, chemist, newsagent, post office and antiques.

TRAINS - sparse local service on the scenic line to Lancaster via Giggleswick with connections southwards to Skipton and Leeds. Tel: 0113-2448133.
BUSES - Pennine Motors to/from Settle and Skipton plus occasional links with Malham (for the tarn, cove, and Gordale Scar). Tel: 01756-749215.

HAPTON
Map 7

Reputedly the first village in England to be provided (in 1888) with domestic electricity, courtesy of a local entrepreneur whose family went on to be early manufacturers of cinematic equipment and magnetos for motor cars. Consisting of two pubs, a fish & chip shop, newsagent, general store and post office, Hapton is now a useful point of disembarkation for boaters to stretch their legs in the long, lockless pound between Blackburn and Burnley. With the benefit of bicycles, you could make an excursion to the neighbouring town of Padiham where Gawthorpe Hall is open to the public.

HEBDEN BRIDGE — Map 29

Hebden's economy no longer relies on the manufacture of fustian, a sort of thick, twilled cloth, but on attracting tourists. There are even New Age overtones which make it appear, at times, like a northern version of Totnes. But in its setting, deep within the wooded folds of the Calder gorge, and in its sturdy, honey-coloured stone buildings, it transcends any tendency to quaintness, whilst there are many fascinating nooks and crannys waiting to be discovered by the diligent explorer.

TYTHE BARN - on A646 overlooking canal east of Mayroyd Mill Lock. Busy, modernised, 'all day' family pub. Boddingtons beer and a wide range of food.

FOX & GOOSE - on A646 at western end of town. Real-ale enthusiasts' pub.

STUBBING WHARF - canalside above Stubbing Locks. Cosy Whitbread pub offering food.

BARGE BRANWELL - tea & coffee from a converted keel, plus canal crafts.

Natwest, Yorkshire, Barclays and Lloyds banks, small market on Thursdays. Food Fair supermarket adjacent to Hebble End, plus heaps of 'quaint' little shops, antiques and second-hand bookshops. Several excellent bakers and butchers.

TRAINS - frequent Calder Valley service connecting with Sowerby Bridge and Todmorden, good for towpath walks. Tel: 0113-244-8133.

BUSES - Yorkshire Rider services duplicate the rail corridor but also offer panoramic journeys up over t'moors to Burnley and Keighley etc. Tel: 01422-365985.

(i) TOURIST INFORMATION - Bridge Gate. Tel: 01422-843831.

HONEY BEE WORLD - Hebble End Works (canalside). Everything you ever wanted to know about bees, plus adjoining craft workshops. Tel: 01422-845557 .

WALKLEY CLOGS - canalside east of Falling Royd Tunnel. Everything you ever wanted to know about clog making, plus specialist craft and retail outlets and childrens' "Enchanted Wood". Tel: 01422-842061.

AUTOMOBILIA - Old Town. Museum of old cars, motorcycles and bicycles. Open Sundays throughout the year, plus Tue, Thur & Fri in summer. Tel: 01422-844775.

CALDER VALLEY CRUISING - The Marina. Tel: 01422-845557. Regular tug trips as well as horse-drawn excursions to Walkleys and 'themed' cruises.

HUDDERSFIELD — Map 26A

Famous as the adopted 'home' of Handel's "Messiah", 'Huddy' reminds you of an old coat, long since replaced by smarter, more expensive garments, that you can't bring yourself to part with. The metaphor isn't entirely contrived, for there is a comfortable reassurance about the dignified Victorian thoroughfares of Huddersfield which has regrettably been exorcised by more get up and go places with their ghastly shopping malls and gratuitous chain store mentality. The same mentality - more's the pity - which has rendered Aspley Basin, terminus of the Huddersfield Broad Canal, so neat and yet so bland. Better, for once, to come by train and begin your exploration of this wonderful town beneath the massive Corinthan portico of the railway station.

THE ASPLEY - Aspley Basin. Modern "Brewers Fayre" pub ideal for families.

THE BLUE ROOMS - Byram Arcade (Westgate). Open Mon-Sat. Superb wholefood restaurant and coffee house tucked away at the rear of a two storey Victorian aracde. A tendency to become crowded at lunchtime, so get there as early as you can.

Excellent shopping centre in streets still laid out in a human, as opposed to car, friendly pattern where the specialist retailers can still afford the rents to rub shoulders with the big boys. Memorable pork pies (best eaten warm in Yorkshire style) from Mitchell's butcher shop in Station Street.

TRAINS - frequent services to major Pennine centres. Useful link with Mirfield for walks along The Broad. Tel: 0113-244-8133.

(i) TOURIST INFORMATION - Albion Street. Tel: 01484-430808.

ART GALLERY - Central Library.

KEIGHLEY

Map 15

Unexpectedly substantial town lurking a mile across the Aire from the canal at Stockbridge. Revered in beer drinking circles as the home of Timothy Taylor's prize-winning ales, and amongst railway enthusiasts as the junction for the Worth Valley Railway, which will carry you up into Bronteland and the haunts of "The Railway Children". Canalside, STOCKBRIDGE and RIDDLESDEN offer typical suburban facilities: some corner shops, one or two pubs, fish & chips and a handy launderette. Thus it's strange to come upon, in such surroundings, the National Trust's EAST RIDDLESDEN HALL, a 17th century manor house and tithe barn surrounded by fishponds. Open Easter to October (though not daily) further details can be had on 01535-607075.

KILDWICK

Map 14

Charming village 'twinned' with Farnhill on the opposite bank of the canal. Good spot to moor overnight with a pleasant pub (THE WHITE LION) where families are welcome and food is available lunchtimes and evenings. FARNHILL STORES provide useful basic provisions if you're caught with an empty larder between the supermarkets of Skipton and Silsden.

LEEDS

Map 19

Having been wooed and won by the riverfront, we were in the mood to like Leeds, and it didn't let us down. If Manchester (as we've said elsewhere) is the great plutocrat of the North, Leeds is its sleek mistress. A class act, endowed with busty public buildings, notably the Town Hall and the Corn Exchange, both designed by local architect, Cuthbert Broderick, in the middle of the nineteenth century when Leeds was bareback riding to prominence on the back of the Industrial Revolution, making household names of Hudswell Clarke, Kitsons, Fowlers and their ilk. Likewise, Leeds reinvented itself during the financial boom at the end of the 1980s, and as a centre of finance (or credit as they deftly call it these days) it claims to rival London. And so wandering in to the centre, we found a city apparently 'pleased as Punch' with itself, wheeling and dealing its way through another buying and selling day; its populace whooping up Briggate and whirling along The Headrow like leaves in an Autumn gale. Their enthusiasm - whatever the cause, however misplaced - was infectious, and we loved every minute of our stay in the headquarters of Tykeland.

GRANARY CAFE - Granary Wharf. Light snacks in the Dark Arches.
THE ADELPHI - adjacent south end of Leeds Bridge. Wonderfully ornate city bar of Edwardian origin. Lunchtime food on weekdays, Tetley beer pumped, we wondered, direct from the brewery?
WHITELOCKS - Turks Head Yard, Briggate. A richer, more bedazzling version of "The Adelphi" and slightly more self conscious, but well worth patronising, especially for Younger's No.3. Food, but not on Sun eves.
SPARROWS WHARF - riverside, The Calls. Warehouse conversion on north bank of Aire downstream of Leeds Bridge. Good value lunches - you pay at the bar and take a token to the hatch. Taylor's on tap.
POOL COURT AT 42 - riverside by Calls Bridge. Gastronomically, ambiently and financially sophisticated restaurant; perfect antidote to a hard day on the river. Tel: 0113-244-4242. Aperitifs on a balcony over the Aire. Closed on Suns and Sat lunchtime. Less formal adjunct in BRASSERIE 44.
Leeds likes to remind you that it was the birthplace of Marks & Spencer. But they've come a long way since the Penny Bazaar, and this is now one of the great shopping centres of the North, commercially and topographically refined; a far cry from the treadmills of Meadowhall. Of course you may get no further than GRANARY WHARF itself, a development of craft shops and the like in the vaults below the railway station. But you should press on: to the VICTORIA QUARTER , a trio of aracdes where you begin to wonder if an employee of Barings Bank has somehow tapped in to your credit account; to KIRKGATE MARKET, a typically splendid northern indoor market hall; to the eliptically-shaped and domed CORN EXCHANGE with its specialist outlets and open-plan cafes; or to QUEENS COURT, a neighbouring caravanserai of nicky-nacky-noo shops in an 18th century cloth merchant's house.
TRAINS - city station is just three minutes walk from Granary Wharf. Tel: 0113-244-8133. BUSES - Tel: 0113-245-7676.
TOURIST INFORMATION - City Station. Tel: 0113-247-8301.
ARMLEY MILLS - canalside bridge 225. Tel: 0113-263-7861. Open daily (ex Mon). Displays of Leeds's industrial history.
THWAITE MILLS - canalside below Knostrop Fall Lock (Map 20). Tel: 0113-249-6453. Open daily (ex Mon). Restored watermill.
KIRKSTALL ABBEY - 10 minutes walk from bridge 221A (Map 18). Tel: 0113-275-5821. Ruined abbey and museum of domestic history featuring reconstructed Victorian street and shops.
TETLEY'S BREWERY WHARF - Waterfront, Calls Bridge. Tel: 0113-242-0666. The history of brewing as seen through the eye of Tetley's marketing department.

LITTLEBOROUGH

Map 31

A traveller in the days before the canal or railway came to Littleborough, found it "a very desirable retreat when it is found impossible to ascend the mountains, during the continuance of the howling storm." Nothing much has changed, for there is still an inclination to sit tight in Littleborough, waiting for the skies to clear before tackling the summit.

FALCON INN - old coaching inn located on A58.

THE RAILWAY - basic Bass local overlooking the nemisis of navigation.

THE SUMMIT - cosy pub adjacent to western end of canal summit. Thwaites beer, bar & restaurant meals.

Surprisingly extensive facilities including: LO-COST supermarket adjacent to railway station. Nat West, Barclays and Yorkshire banks. Antiquarian bookshop. Launderette on Victoria Street.

TRAINS - half-hourly Calder Valley link with Todmorden and Rochdale; (hourly with Walsden). Tel: 0161-832-8353.

COACH HOUSE HERITAGE CENTRE - Tel: 01706-78481. Closed Mondays. Exhibitions of Littleborough's history and tearooms.

MIRFIELD

Map 25

"A useful place to get supplies" according to one waterway guide, which is like saying: "Meryl Streep, quite a good actress." But if you don't look you don't see, and we fell hook, line and sinker for Mirfield; aided and abetted by the pony-tailed girl behind the counter at Chapman's corner shop, who serves hot corned-beef and baked-bean pies with the smile of a PreRaphaelite angel. And don't they know that Charlotte Bronte was educated (and later taught) here; and didn't they fall for the post-woollen beauty of South Brook and Ledgard mills; and didn't they catch sight of one of Mirfield's own Longstaff double-deckers filling with workers at dawn; and didn't they walk up the asphalt lane to pay homage to the old engine sheds? A "useful place" indeed!

THE NAVIGATION - canalside Station Road. Homely inn set back from canal bank offering Bass and John Smith's beers and lunches. Families welcome.

THE SHIP - Shepley Bridge. "Brewers Fayre" family pub overlooking unnavigable reach of the Calder.

CALDER ROAD FISHERIES - mouthwatering fish & chips (not Mon/Tue eves) south of bridge 17 beyond the railway bridge.

Even the Co-op FOOD FAIR (8am-8pm Mon-Sat) sells corned-beef and baked-bean pie, though it's not as succulent as CHAPMANS on the corner of Calder Road south of the railway from bridge 17. Banks include: Barclays, Midland and Nat West.

TRAINS - frequent connections with Wakefield, Leeds & Huddersfield.

NELSON

Map 9

The story goes that Nelson, formerly known as Marsden, got its new name when the Lancashire & Yorkshire Railway company tired of passengers ending up at Marsden (Yorks) when they really wanted to be in Marsden (Lancs). You wonder how they knew the difference! But anyway Marsden turned itself into Nelson and never looked back, becoming quite a large cotton town towards the end of the nineteenth century, and quite a large administrative centre, for the Borough of Pendle, towards the end of the twentieth. Overlooked by a Pendle Hill sugar-iced with snow, we moored by the Palatine Working Mens Club opposite Yarnspinners Wharf (so they're good story tellers here, eh?) and made our way up Pendle Street between a mosque and Mellins butcher's shop (whose black pudding, taken back to the boat and served warm with hot dogs, melts in your mouth) to the centre of town; a windswept, pedestrianised area apparently modelled (not entirely successfully) on Moscow's Red Square.

TRAINS - local services along the Colne-Burnley line. Tel: 01772-259439.

TOURIST INFORMATION - Town Hall. Tel: 01282-692890.

PENDLE WAVELENGTHS - Leeds Road. Tel: 01282-693287. "Tropical indoor paradise."

RISHTON

Map 6

Large village with a tendency to dourness but offering some useful small shops for passing canallers.

- CANAL BRIDGE CAFE - hot meals for hungry boaters.
- THE ROEBUCK - 18th century coaching inn.
- Midland & TSB banks. Greengrocers and chemist, post office, newsagent and general stores. Gift shop.

SALTAIRE

Map 16

In the good old days you could get to Saltaire by trolleybus crammed with millworkers. Now it's on the tourist map, and Bradford's trolleybus network - though the last in Britain to lower its poles - ceased operating in 1972. But however you come here now, the journey's still worth the making, for though spruced-up beyond all recognition, and no longer wrapped in a pall of worsted cloth mill chimney smoke, Saltaire is still intact and recognisably as its creator, mid nineteenth century mill owner and philanthropist, Sir Titus Salt, intended it to be. Moreover, the lotus-eaters are catered for without obvious detriment to the environment or, in other words, Saltaire's soul remains its own. And, in any case, if the Italianate streets of dignified stone terraces, named after Sir Titus's children, become too oppressively busy, you can always escape by cable car up the enchanted glen to Baildon Moor beyond.

- BEETIES - Victoria Road, adjacent bridge 207A. Charming basement tea rooms with adjoining restaurant (Tel: 01274-595988). Tasty food and a good atmosphere put it in our 'top six'.
THE BOATHOUSE - riverside by bridge 207A. Quaint, licensed - teetotal Titus would not have approved!
SALTS DINER - Salts Mill. Informal cafe on second floor of gigantic mill.
VICTORIA FISHERIES - adjacent bridge 207A. Eat in or take-away fish & chips as only Yorkshire knows how.
- Shop till you drop in Saltaire's array of consumer age honey-pots: antiques, clothes, textiles, crafts, gifts and books. A personal favourite is THE BODHRAN on Victoria Street where there's a Celtic bias to the books and music on sale. More practically, there's a SPAR grocery on Titus Street, and a post office and branches of Lloyds and Barclays banks up on the A650; though to find a friendly cash-point you needs must travel to Shipley.
- TRAINS - frequent services along the newly electrified Aire Valley line to/from Skipton, Leeds and Bradford. Tel: 0113-244-8133.

- (i) 1853 GALLERY - Ground Floor, Salts Mill. Exhibits include premier collection of local artist made good, David Hockney.
ORGAN & HARMONIUM MUSEUM - Victoria Road. Open daily ex Fri & Sat. 11am-4pm.
SHIPLEY GLEN TRAMWAY - 5 minutes stroll across the Aire from bridge 207A. Victorian cable tramway revelling in its centenary in 1995. Slightly complex operating schedule, but usually open daily throughout the summer plus winter weekends. Tel: 01274-589010. Charming small funfair for children at the top and romantic walks up on t'tops.

SHIPLEY

Map 16

Shipley sulks in the penumbra cast by Saltaire's film star looks; though it is not without a certain sullen charm of its own. Our usually resourceful research crew even had difficulty in locating a shop enterprising enough to sell them Sunday papers. As we remarked in our Settle & Carlisle railway guide, the Arndale Shopping Centre is "so architecturally abhorent that it is almost charming", but boaters may find it of some practical use in the otherwise shopless void southwards to Leeds and northwards to Bingley. Quite the best thing about Shipley if you haven't brought your own boat with you, is the WATERBUS service provided by Apollo Cruisers on a regular basis between here and Bingley. Telephone 01274-595914 for further details. Failing that, catch the first train out to Bradford or Ilkley.

SILSDEN

Map 14

Behind the slightly grim counterance of mills and factories, Silsden proves to be a surprisingly pleasant little town (or should that be, large village) attractively watered by a tributary of the Aire which skips along the High Street like a happy child.

- BRIDGE INN - canalside bridge 191A. Delightful pub which actually pre-dates the canal, harking back as far as the 17th century. Bar meals and Masham's own "Black Sheep" ale on tap. Families catered for. Exceptionally good FISH & CHIP shop next door.
- Useful little shopping centre with NatWest & Barclays banks. Several good old fashioned retailers like HILLS the baker and HOLGATES the grocer.
- TRAINS - station (Steeton & Silsden) lies a mile south-west of canal but there are bus or taxi connections Tel: 0113-244-8133.

SKIPTON

Map 13

Is Skipton the perfect, medium-sized town? Quite possibly yes! Self-styled as the "Gateway to the Dales", old 'Sheep Town' holds sway over the Aire Gap as it has done since the 7th century. We liked it so much that we kept making tenuous excuses to go back and check this or that, putting up at "Randells" comfortable canalside hotel, sipping a cocktail or two on the terrace, whilst other boaters put their backs into the neighbouring swingbridge. The growth of familiarity bred a deepening affection for the town: from its broad, typically Yorkshire High Street - pulsating with market stalls on most days - to quieter, more intimate ginnels and courtyards, topographically estranged from the main thoroughfares in aloof oases of timeless calm.

BLACK HORSE HOTEL - High Street. Old coaching inn used for meetings by the L&L's promoters. Tel: 01756-792145.
ROYAL SHEPHERD - Canal Street. Charming muzak-free town pub overlooking Springs Branch Arm offering lunches, a peaceful garden, stained-glass with a canal theme, and an interesting range of authentic ales.
BIZZIE LIZZIES - canalside (bridge 178) fish restaurant.
EASTWOODS - ditto (bridge 179A).
WATERSIDE COTTAGE - Coach Street. Busy canalside tea rooms.
RANDELLS - canalside hotel at Snaygill (bridge 181) with hospitable lounge bar offering light meals throughout the day as well as a more elaborate restaurant. Tel: 01756-700100.
BAY HORSE - canalside at Snaygill (bridge 182). Solid, traditional Tetley pub with family room, garden and steak restaurant.

Shopping is Skipton's strongpoint and it has attracted the likes of Rackhams, Laura Ashley and the Edinburgh Woolen Mill to open branches here. The market flourishes on most weekdays. Many alleyways slink furtively away from the main street and issue into interesting courtyards, most notably CRAVEN COURT which, from a narrow entry, opens out into an airy rectangle covered by a graceful canopy of cast iron and glass. Sooner or later, though, most folk end up at STANFORTH'S, the "celebrated pork pie establishment", handily located for canal users by bridge 2 on the Spring's Branch, where the pies come warm, Yorkshire fashion, and the jelly 'explodes' in your mouth (and all down your clothes if you're not careful). Most banks have branches in the town and there are TESCO and MORRISONS supermarkets within easy reach of the canal.

TRAINS - excellent service southwards to Leeds and Bradford with handy stops along the Aire Valley for towpath walkers. Skipton can also be used as a launch pad for the Settle & Carlisle if you've time at your disposal. Tel: 0113-244-8133.
BUSES - Pennine run to Gargrave, Barnoldswick, Colne and Burnley. Tel: 01756-749215.
(i) TOURIST INFORMATION - Sheep Street. Tel: 01756-792809.
SKIPTON CASTLE - The town's crowning glory. Superb 11th century fortification, though much domesticised down the years. Open daily from 10am (2pm Sundays). Tel: 01756-792442.
EMBSAY STEAM RAILWAY - located at Embsay two miles east of town centre (bus connections). Delightful small steam line in the process of extending to Bolton Abbey. Tel: 01756-794727 for operating details.
PENNINE BOAT TRIPS - Coach Street. Public trips and charters by wideboat, an excellent taster for the L&L if you're not already afloat. Tel: 01756-790829.

SOWERBY BRIDGE

Map 28

For some reason, hard to fathom, Sowerby Bridge reminded us of Domodossola in the Italian Alps. Perhaps it was the boulder-strewn riverbed; or an empathetic similarity in the high buildings of indigenous stone, stacked precariously upon each other as if on the shelves on an untidy warehouse; or that same, slightly lugubrious sense of a workaday town hewn from a mountain fastness. But when we tried our hesitant Italian on the check-out girl at Kwik Save we got no response; though do you ever?